4

Increase Yo[ur]
3 MINUTES a Day

ACT
Essay

RANDALL MCCUTCHEON AND JAMES SCHAFFER, PH.D.

McGraw·Hill

New York   Chicago   San Francisco   Lisbon   London   Madrid   Mexico City
Milan   New Delhi   San Juan   Seoul   Singapore   Sydney   Toronto

Library of Congress Cataloging-in-Publication Data

McCutcheon, Randall, 1949–
    Increase your score in 3 minutes a day. ACT essay / Randall McCutcheon, James
Schaffer.
       p.   cm.
    ISBN 0-07-145666-X
    1. English language—Composition and exercises—Examinations—Study
guides.   2. ACT Assessment—Study guides.   I. Title: Increase your score in
three minutes a day. ACT essay.   II. Title: ACT essay.   III. Schaffer, James,
1949–. IV. Title.

LB1631.5.M32   2005
378.1′662—dc22   2005043767

ISBN 0-07-145666-X

Interior design by Cheryl McLean
Interior illustrations:
Page xii by David Ernest Lyon; page 8 © The New Yorker Collection 1987 J. B. Handelsman
from cartoonbank.com. All rights reserved; page 16 © 2003 ZITS Partnership. Reprinted
with special permission of King Features Syndicate; pages 37 and 53 © 1974. Peanuts
reprinted by permission of United Feature Syndicate, Inc.; page 64 © 1972. Peanuts
reprinted by permission of United Feature Syndicate, Inc.; page 82 © The New Yorker
Collection 2001 Danny Shanahan from cartoonbank.com. All rights reserved; page 92 ©
Sidney Harris. Reprinted with permission; page 111 © 1998 ZITS Partnership. Reprinted
with special permission of King Features Syndicate; page 116 Calvin and Hobbes © 1993
Watterson. Reprinted with permission of Universal Press Syndicate. All rights reserved.

McGraw-Hill books are available at special quantity discounts to use as premiums and
sales promotions, or for use in corporate training programs. For more information, please
write to the Director of Special Sales, Professional Publishing, McGraw-Hill, Two Penn
Plaza, New York, NY 10121-2298. Or contact your local bookstore.

Also in this series

Increase Your Score in 3 Minutes a Day: ACT Reading, McCutcheon and Schaffer
Increase Your Score in 3 Minutes a Day: SAT Critical Reading, McCutcheon and Schaffer
Increase Your Score in 3 Minutes a Day: SAT Essay, McCutcheon and Schaffer

This book is printed on acid-free paper.

····················

For my grandmother.
—Randall McCutcheon

····································

*To Mary Lynn, for her unwavering love
and support, and to Suzanne, Sarah, and
Stephen, who make it all worthwhile.*
—James Schaffer

Contents

Foreword

Memoirs of a Grammarian

Professional writers know a secret. I'll tell it to you right now so you can skip years of ineffective writing and get directly to the effective stuff. Here goes:

Context is everything.

I know it doesn't sound like much, but you'd be surprised how few people, even very literate people, understand it. That beautiful passage you think about so often? Probably it isn't beautiful because of the writer's choice of words so much as because it draws together, and draws upon, the material that comes before it. Writing effectively isn't all that much different from telling a good joke. Rambling along during the setup only makes the punch line less punchy.

Here's another thing about context: the way you write depends on what you're writing. Advertising copy doesn't read like a novel. A novel doesn't read like a corporate report—or at least a good one doesn't.

I'm sure that right now the ACT essay makes the short list of threatening and unavoidable ordeals looming in your immediate future. Fortunately you are holding in your hand a book that, while it may not succeed in making the essay any more avoidable, can certainly make it less threatening. It is filled with reliable advice about keeping your essay on track, ensuring that things go well together, and choosing an approach suited to the task you're undertaking—in short, about being mindful of context. That, after all, is the key to effective writing.

And remember this: no matter how bleak things look, you'll still have it better than I did. I needed nine years and two discarded 750-page drafts to write *Memoirs of a Geisha*. Your struggle, on the other hand, will draw to a close no more than a few hours after it begins. Sigh.

Anyway, it's a good thing you have this wise and useful book to help you with it. So what are you waiting for? You've got some reading to do.

—Arthur Golden, author of
Memoirs of a Geisha

Acknowledgments

The authors would like to thank the following people:
Jane Durso, Peter Durso, Elizabeth Durso, Nick Durso, Matthew Barrett, Amaris Singer, Ladan Jafari, Molly Dunn, Yasmin Mashhoon, Reah Johnson, Austan Goolsbee, Jeremy Mallory, Christopher Brown, Mary Schafer, Thomas Schaffer, Mel Bakke, Megan Cimpl, Kelly Douglas, Kari Fisk, Josh Fox, Jody Friesen, Jeff Gilbreath, Katie Goebel, Justin Haag, Jason Hietbrink, Steph Keeler, Amanda Kershner, Jenn Koester, Jean-David Lassy, Byron Lefler, Jill McCann, Rosemary Melnarik, Stephen Meredith, Anne Meyers, Jeff Moors, Andrea Kaminski, Nikki Mosier, Jess Nielsen, Darshan Patel, Phil Pelster, Libby Peters, Brock Pillen, Matt Prokop, Abby Shreve, Seth Svendsen, Ryan Sweeny, Shawn Votava, Connor White, Geoff Weller, and Angie Workman.

Introduction

*"If we listened to our intellect, we'd never have a love affair.
We'd never have a friendship. We'd never go into business,
because we'd be too cynical. Well, that's nonsense. You've
got to jump off cliffs all the time and build your wings
on the way down."*

—Ray Bradbury

tart flapping. Bradbury is right; this is no time for cynicism. A leap of faith is called for. A belief in yourself. The ACT essay is nothing more than a thirty-minute writing test, after all.

Richard Ferguson, Chief Executive Officer of ACT, says: "By offering the ACT Writing Test as an option, we are providing a flexible solution rather than imposing a single approach on all students and institutions."

Ha ha. Unless you are forbidden to do so by a particular college—and that's not going to happen—sign up for the writing test. Think of it as a "measly" vaccination that inoculates you against suspicious admissions officers. If you aren't willing to submit a writing sample, they may well wonder, what weaknesses are you trying to hide? And, perhaps, did Mom really write that compelling application essay you sent in? More than two million students must face this addition, this rite of passage, each year. You, for example. Is this a fair measure of your potential? Hmm . . . As a high school student, University of Chicago professor Austan Goolsbee wrote that a standardized test should have one judging criterion: "It should be more than a meaningless rite. It should be educationally right."

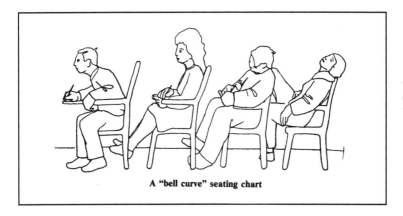

A "bell curve" seating chart

Goolsbee was on to something. Teachers of writing must battle bravely against formulaic writing. But how? Peggy Hill, on the animated television show "King of the Hill," echoed the battle cry of most contemporary writing teachers: "You do not come into my house and correct my grammar unless your name is Strunk or White."

Clearly, the classic *Elements of Style* is more revered than any book of its kind. And you could do far worse than worshipping this "geriatric" text. The book you are reading never strays far from the teachings of William Strunk Jr. and E. B. White. After all, the person who reads your essay will reward the clear and correct writing prescribed in *Elements*.

The truth is, lively writing comes from more than simply following the rules. White himself admitted to writing by ear. He knew that expressiveness is not always about exactness. It is more often about taking risks. O frabjous day.

In the *New Yorker*, Adam Lehner spoofed the advice of Strunk and White.

Blessed are the verbose in spirit, for theirs shall be the kingdom of clarity; the inheritance of the ability to name those children who sat beside them in third grade, and of the ability to name many animals, in a singular minute, is what's coming to those who use complicated grammar.

Once again truth trumps fiction. In a 1982 study, Hunter Breland and Robert Jones of the Educational Testing Service (ETS) found that "verbosity" was more important in achieving high scores than such other essay characteristics as "sentence logic," "supporting materials," and "precision of diction." David Owen, who discusses this research in his book *None of the Above*, suggests that test takers should also remember to indent. Evidently, most readers like lots of paragraphs, too.

Of course, much time has passed since the Breland and Jones study. Changes have been implemented. The ACT assures students that these essays will be graded by experienced high school and college English teachers.

Jane Mallison, a reader of standardized test essays for more than twenty years, compared the scoring of the essays to judging beef stew at the county fair. She said:

> *You're not grading the beef. You're not grading the sauce.*
> *You're not grading the herbs. You're grading the whole stew.*

This book, then, is about the stew, the whole stew, and nothing but the stew.

Making This Book Work for You

∙∙∙

We didn't exaggerate. You can significantly improve your chances for a higher score on the ACT by studying this book for three minutes a day. OK, we exaggerated slightly. Conscientious students (and slow readers) may want to invest a few more minutes each day. Practice and review. Practice and review.

If you're a high school student on the go (and what high school student isn't?), you could download some new software on your cell phone. The software offers about six hundred practice questions and test-taking strategies for the ACT. In a gamelike feature, users can compete against a clock, against other players, or even across the Internet.

A better bet (and a cheaper one) is to make the most of this book. In the next few pages you'll learn about several different approaches—ways to get the most out of your studying, depending on how much time you have before the test.

In the meantime, however, be sure to consider the single best plan for doing well on the ACT—take tough classes. As Richard Ferguson, ACT's CEO, puts it, "Not only is the number of courses important, but the quality and intensity of these classes will determine if a high school student is ready for college and work." So tough it out.

By the way, ACT no longer stands for American College Testing, though it once did. As the company expanded its programs to include work skills tests and professional certification, it changed its name: ACT is no longer an acronym (a bunch of letters that stand for a series of words); it's just the company's name.

The Basic Approach
The Eight-Week, Three-Minutes-a-Day Plan

Day 1: Study the "Introduction" and "Making This Book Work for You" sections.

Days 2–31: Study one writing principle each day. These principles will help you to answer the multiple-choice questions as well as help you to prepare to write the essay. Then, three times throughout the day, review—in your head—the essential ideas taught in that day's principle. The next morning—in the shower—say aloud those same essential ideas. Repeat. And not just the shampoo. Lather too.

Days 32–41: Begin mastering the test strategies. Use the same daily routine that you practiced with the writing principles—one strategy each day.

Days 42–53: Read one practice essay example each day. Study the comments of the grader. Think carefully about the insights provided for each essay.

Days 54–56: Spend one more day on each of the three best essays. Brainstorm different ways that you could implement the characteristics of those essays in the development of various topics.

Day 57: Celebrate. Take as long as you like.

The Advanced Approach

Even a student lost in the bewilderness of the ACT can figure out that the Basic Approach—small masterpiece that it is—falls short of what is really needed. To adequately prepare for the ACT essay, you have to practice writing. You must apply the writing principles and test strategies by writing your own practice essays—the more the merrier (at least on the day you get your ACT score in the mail).

So what should you do? First, follow the Basic Approach. Now add time for applying what you've learned each day in an actual piece of writing. The piece of writing can be the homework you're already doing or an e-mail to a friend or a polite note to your probation officer. But write with purpose. Tiger Woods doesn't just hit golf balls at the driving range. He practices with every club in his bag. And, more important, he always aims at a specific target.

Tiger's goal is to play with his A game. What about you? What is your goal? And that concludes your first *lessen*.

The Last-Minute Approach . . . or ACT-CPR

You've procrastinated. The ACT is only a week away. How do you resuscitate your chances for essay success? Our prescription: choose one of the following two protocols.

Protocol 1: Skip the writing principles and test strategies sections. Turn to the six practice essay topics. Spend the minutes you've allocated for study on one of the topics each day. Pay special attention to the comments of the grader and to the annotations provided. On the seventh day, rest and review.

Protocol 2: This protocol requires additional time each day but is a more thorough "treatment." Thus, the prognosis for recovery is better. On the first two days, study the writing principles section. On the next two days, study the test strategies section. Work on three of the practice essays for each of the next two days. On the seventh day, rest and review.

What is that word that a doctor shouts when an emergency room patient goes into cardiac arrest? Oh yeah, "Clear."

CLEAR!

Good news. You have a pulse. So defibril . . . later. Study now.

WRITING PRINCIPLES

Three minutes a day is just enough time to brush your teeth, glance over the sports section of the paper, or boot up your computer.

Three minutes a day is also all the time you'll need to learn an important writing principle. In just three minutes (and with a little practice) you can learn why some grammar "truths" are myths, how to cut the clutter out of your writing, and how to make one sentence flow seamlessly into another.

Devote just three minutes a day to each of the principles in this section and you will soon find yourself a more thoughtful and skilled writer. These principles are not just another version of the nearly endless chain of grammar guidebooks. Those books offer a long series of *don'ts*.

Instead, the principles in this section offer lots of *dos*. Do put the most important word at the end of the sentence, do vary the length of your sentences, and do use an occasional metaphor.

So dedicate yourself to a daily three-minute workout. Pump some heavy vocabulary, lift a few semicolons, press a dash, and bench a simile. Easier than a session on the treadmill or stair-climber, these simple, three-minute lessons will bring a new level of fitness to your prose.

The ACT Scars
You for Life

Hyperbole. The world's largest ball of string. The world's longest deli sandwich. The world's cranberry capital. We've all heard these claims before. Perhaps your town describes itself as the world's greatest _____ (fill in the blank). No harm done, right? And maybe even a few unsuspecting tourists drop by.

In writing, however, overblown exaggerations quickly erode an ACT reader's faith. Make modest claims. When you write statements that include the words *always*, *every*, or *all*, you make readers grit their teeth. For example, do you feel yourself silently thinking, "Yeah, right" when you read the following:

I never procrastinate.

I always eat healthy.

Everyone should study economics.

Remember the story about the boy who cried wolf. Beware the false alarm.

Young writers are often tempted to exaggerate in the one place where modesty and humility are most becoming: the thesis statement. Imagine a student who was assigned to write an essay on the Lewis and Clark expedition and, much to the student's dismay, more specifically, the prairie dog.

Mystified at how to generate more than a sentence or two on the annoying little pest, he or she pumped some hot air into the thesis, hoping, perhaps, to make the essay seem more important:

> *The prairie dog had a huge impact on the Lewis and Clark expedition. The prairie dog was the species that fascinated and impacted the expedition members more than any other animal.*

This thesis statement is far too grand. Why claim the prairie dog was the most important animal? It wasn't a source of food (such as the buffalo) or a source of fear (the grizzly).

The fact is, you don't need to make a huge claim to have a good thesis. Something simpler, such as "The prairie dog was one of many new animal species that fascinated Lewis and other members of the expedition. The way Lewis studied this creature reveals much about his attitudes toward science and nature," would work well. More important, it wouldn't alienate the kind of ACT readers who are going to dig in their heels and say, "Prove it, buster."

Exaggerating is only human. Consider any angler you've ever met. But just as we keep our skepticism when it comes to fish stories, we are usually alert for any claim that asks too much.

If you want to be believed, go easy on the hyperbole. Those tiny white lies may seem harmless to you, but readers don't like having their legs pulled.

Debunking Grammar Myths

rammar myths sometimes get in the way of graceful prose. The laws of grammar come and go. We make up rules when we need them and throw them away when we don't.

We've all heard, for example, that we should never use contractions such as *don't* or *won't* in formal writing. Poppycock! Contractions can be both graceful and conversational. We should use them whenever they sound better than writing out the words.

Here are three other common but flawed assumptions that should no longer stifle your writing.

1. **Incomplete sentences are incorrect.** Writers often use incomplete sentences. According to Richard Lederer, author of *Anguished English*, many professional writers begin up to one-tenth of their sentences with conjunctions such as *and* and *but*. Your concern, therefore, should not be with incomplete sentences but with incomplete thoughts.

   In the hands of skillful writers, sentence fragments can perk up prose, making it less stiff and formal. They can also create a nice dynamic with long sentences. Call it, in author Constance Hale's phrase, "pause and effect." For example:

   "Man is the only animal that blushes. Or needs to."
   —Mark Twain

   Over the years, some English teachers have enforced the notion that *and* and *but* should be used to join elements within a sentence, not to join one sentence with another. Not so. It has been common practice to begin sentences with them since at least as far back as the tenth century. But don't overdo it or your writing will sound monotonous.

2. **Sentences should not start with *there*.** Admittedly, this construction means that the reader won't know the subject at first, but never to begin a sentence with *there* is a mistake. *There* is there to set the stage for what is to come. Use too many sentences, however, that start with "There is" or "There are," and your writing loses energy.

3. **Sentences should not end with a preposition.** Here is another bugaboo that English teachers used to get worked up over. Author Patricia T. O'Connor credits an eighteenth-century grammar book for setting the precedent that somehow caught on with the public. Nobody knows why grammarians insist on living in the past. Writers don't.

   Winston Churchill in one of his witty moments remarked, "A preposition is something you should never end a sentence with." If the prime minister of England can do it, so can you. Just remember that breaking the rules can lead to breakthrough prose.

Think About the Reader First

Writers have many different ways of thinking about the people who will read their work. Some imagine an ideal reader—someone who would read with interest and enthusiasm; some imagine a close friend or relative; some even imagine a disagreeable person who would be likely to find fault at every turn. In each case, having an image in mind of a potential reader helps the writer find the right words to use.

Pretend for a moment that your classmates are your audience for something you're going to write. What do you know about them? Can you guess their average age, number of brothers and sisters, favorite hobbies, possessions, interests, and pastimes? How can you describe their attitudes toward school, jobs, popular music, cars, and clothes? What would they be most interested in knowing about you?

Professional writers must often think carefully about the people who are most likely to read what they are writing. Writers take what those readers like and dislike into consideration as they work. The typical ACT reader is probably an experienced English teacher.

When considering that reader, ask yourself these questions:

- Is my choice of subject appropriate?
- Am I giving my reader new information? Anything he or she doesn't know already?
- Is my material too difficult or too easy?
- How can I connect my message with my reader's interests?

Don't talk to the ACT reader as if he or she is a stranger or somehow beneath you. Consider the reader a sympathetic person who is likely to be interested in anything you find interesting.

Most of all, get off to a good start. The first few words you write often determine whether a reader will stick around. Make your first sentence intriguing, perhaps like these:

- Fourth down and inches to go.
- As a scientist, Throckmorton knew that if he were ever to break wind in the echo chamber he would never hear the end of it.
- I want to die peacefully in my sleep like my grandfather . . . not screaming and yelling in terror like the passengers in his car.

Use your first sentence to set up a problem, to present two sides of a conflict, or to pose a question. Make it impossible, in short, for an ACT reader to quit reading.

"I wish you would make up your mind, Mr. Dickens. Was it the best of times or was it the worst of times? It could scarcely have been both."

One Idea per Sentence

English is getting more and more efficient. That's the conclusion someone fishing for trout might draw upon picking up a copy of *The Compleat Angler* in a local bookstore. *The Compleat Angler*, one of the most popular books of 1653 (OK, maybe there weren't many books in 1653), offers lots of useful tips, such as this:

> *Take this for a rule: When you fish for a Trout with a worm, let your line have so much, and not more lead than will fit the stream in which you fish; that is to say, more in a great troublesome stream than in a smaller that is quieter; as near as may be, so much as will sink the bait to the bottom, and keep it still in motion, and not more.*

The author, Sir Izaak Walton, packs several ideas into a single sentence. We can unpack those ideas—and put them into several sentences—to make our communication more efficient and to help make our angler's life a little easier. For example:

> *If you're going trout fishing, make sure the line you use fits the stream. For example, you'll need a heavier line in a deep river with a strong current. Cast your line in such a way that the bait will sink to the bottom. Then keep the bait slightly in motion, in order to attract the fish you hope to catch.*

A reader would likely have a better shot at a rainbow trout with the modern description. That description, by the way, works because the writer has used only one idea per sentence.

It's generally a prudent idea to serve the ACT reader just one thought at a time. Try to complete that thought before launching a new one. Consider this sentence from a student essay:

> *The choices we have in the student cafeteria are wonderful and the kitchen is open at convenient times for everyone unless you have classes in the middle of the day which is uncommon here at Wesleyan since Wesleyan students like to get a head start on the day with early morning classes.*

That sentence may not make you hungry, but it probably will keep you breathless. Here's how this sentence might have been written in a less confusing manner:

> *The cafeteria offers students a wide choice of times to eat. Early dining hours, for example, are especially convenient for students with morning classes. Students who choose to eat in the middle of the day may encounter some crowded lines, but few have conflicts with classes at those hours.*

"I came. I saw. I conquered," wrote Julius Caesar, and so should you. Put your faith in declarative sentences and develop your ideas, no matter how complicated, one step at a time.

Hold It Together

D o you ever find yourself being put on hold? Maybe you're trying to order a new pair of Air Max Hyperspeed Supernova shoes from a catalog company, or perhaps you're trying to talk to a busy friend with call waiting. In any event, you find yourself patiently idling, waiting to complete your thought after being interrupted.

The same thing can happen to ACT readers when writers persist in piling word after word between the subject and verb of a sentence. For example:

My brother Louis, whom nobody really likes because he is immature but has to tag along with us anyway, is going to the movie with us tonight.

Some readers may have to go back to the beginning of the sentence to remind themselves who or what the subject was.

Strive to put the main character of the sentence (the subject) as close as possible to the plot (the verb). Nobody's saying that sentences can't be complex and interesting; they can, as long as they're easy to follow. But we shouldn't have to read a sentence twice to get it. For example:

We shortly after that found out who wanted to go water skiing with us.

Find a way to put the doer (the subject, *we*) closer to what's being done (the verb, *found out*):

Soon afterward, we found out who wanted to go water skiing with us.

If subjects and verbs drift too far apart, separated by endless intervening clauses, the reader may give up. Therefore, keep subject and verb together so the reader understands the sentence the first time through. In this sentence, "To get to London we, instead of going over, went under the English Channel," the reader's tendency is to ask "What . . . ?" and possibly quit reading.

Instead, by keeping subject and verb near each other, you ask the reader to cope with just one idea at a time. Hence, "To get to London we went under, not over, the English Channel."

On the ACT essay, you are under pressure to write quickly and briefly, much like newspaper headline writers who have learned to tuck their subjects and verbs in the same bed:

*Surprised Troops Hail the Chief (*The president makes an unannounced visit to troops in Iraq.*)*

*For Survivor, Scars Fading Inside and Out (*An eleven-year-old survives a car crash.*)*

French Keep Up Love-Hate Relationship with America (France and the United States still share common values.*)*

The moral of this story is to place one call at a time; talk directly to the reader and keep talking until you've completed your message. Think of your reader as an answering machine, not someone to put on hold.

Make Sentences Hold Hands

The tail feathers of a dove lie over one another in a tight, interlocking pattern that keeps the dove warm and waterproof. The idea makes a good technique for keeping your sentences waterproof, too, something that will impress anyone who reads your ACT essay.

The issue here is how to connect one sentence to the next. When young writers get together to discuss their work, they often say something like, "I wish my sentences flowed better." What they often mean is that they wish one sentence led to the next in a seamless way, "dovetailing," in other words.

The simplest way to dovetail is to repeat a word from the first sentence in the second, as in this example:

> At the Gap, a basic black sweater ran around $44 plus tax.
> **This sweater** was made of wool, cotton, and a bit of
> cashmere.

A writer can also use a pronoun to refer to a previous sentence:

> At the Gap, a basic black sweater ran around $44 plus tax.
> **This sweater** was made of wool, cotton, and a bit of
> cashmere. **It** had a ribbed neckline, sleeves, and waist.

Sometimes the pronoun can be made into an adjective that connects with a different subject. That enables the second sentence to head off in a new direction:

*In the play Mrs. Ethel Savage is a former actress who is now very old, very rich, and very spiteful. **Her** husband has passed away, and **her** greedy children are searching for the ten million dollars in bonds that Mrs. Savage has hidden.*

You can dovetail in a richer, more complicated way by referencing a concept, often by restating it in slightly different terms:

*As with many musicians, the rap artist frequently has **something to say**. Rap is usually criticized because of **its message** of violence, sex, drugs, and obscenity.*

When a writer masters dovetailing, the results can be breathtaking. Notice how smoothly the sentences in this description from *The Water Is Wide* by Pat Conroy flow together:

Yamacraw is an island off the South Carolina mainland not far from Savannah, Georgia. The island is fringed with the green, undulating marshes of the southern coast; shrimp boats ply the waters around her and fishermen cast their lines along her bountiful shores. Deer cut through her forests in small silent herds. The great southern oaks stand broodingly on her banks. The island and the waters around her teem with life. There is something eternal and indestructible about the tide-eroded shores and the dark, threatening silences of the swamps in the heart of the island. Yamacraw is beautiful because man has not yet had time to destroy this beauty.

That's waterproof writing at its best.

Save the Last Dance

Imagine you are a track coach and you're trying to put together a relay team. Where do you put your fastest runner? Where do you put the slowest? Most coaches, it turns out, follow a formula that goes something like this:

- Your fastest runner goes last.
- Your second-fastest runner goes first.
- The two in-between runners go, that's right, in between.

The idea behind this strategy has relevance for writing. You want to get off to a good start. You want to interest your readers and attract their attention. But you also want to save your best for the end. You want your writing to have a payoff.

So, suppose you have three examples to use in support of a point you are trying to make. You would be wise to save your best example for last. Use your second-best example first, and place the other one, the so-so example, in the middle. Putting your best example last should help you clinch your argument.

Let's take a look at how this might work at the sentence level. The most powerful position in a sentence is the last word. Any word next to a period reverberates because the period is a stop sign. Readers must pause over the last word before they move on; it lingers in their mind. When that word appears at the end of a paragraph, it gains even greater emphasis because of the white space that follows it.

Take a look at these examples from student papers:

Does Austin save the day or does Dr. Evil prevail?

At times shopping can be fun, entertaining, boring, interesting, and comical, but it is always, in one way or another, expensive.

Only Nelly could sing a song about tennis shoes and have it be a hit.

None of these writers is particularly sophisticated or accomplished, and yet all know instinctively how to put a key word at the end of a sentence. This principle even works to humorous effect in this unfortunately worded business memo:

The change in maternity leave benefits during the past year has led to some confusion on many people's parts.

The principle here is plain: save your best for last. In time, this will begin to come naturally to you as you write, but in the meantime, use this principle for a few quick revisions. Look back over a paper you've written and find several key sentences. Reread those sentences and consider whether a little rearrangement might produce a more powerful expression—simply by putting the most important word at the end. Once you have reviewed papers you've already written, rearranging sentences on the ACT essay will become second nature.

And if this principle makes sense to you, perhaps you can help answer a tough question. A familiar billboard says, "Eat, shop, relax." Is that really the right order?

The Long and the Short of It

"Eight new choir robes are currently needed, due to the addition of several new members and to the deterioration of some older ones."

The preceding sentence appeared in an actual church bulletin—we can only hope that it was the robes that were deteriorating and not some of the older choir members. The sentence illustrates rather graphically a syntactical problem; that is, a problem stemming from faulty word order. The person who wrote that sentence did not understand the relationships words have with one another. The clarity of a writer's message depends heavily upon proper word placement.

Writers do their hardest work at the level of the sentence. Sentences can generally be described as either "loose" or "periodic." A loose sentence is one in which the grammar is both simple and straightforward. "I went walking with Fred today" is a loose sentence. The subject and verb appear early, and with no complication.

The opposite of a loose sentence is one in which the complexity of subject-verb-object is not resolved until the end—hence the name *periodic* (or, just before the *period*). When a sentence begins, a reader knows to look for certain things, notably the subject and main verb. If something happens to delay them, like prepositional phrases or independent clauses, tension results. The reader waits in a state of suspense. Consider this sentence:

Why you hardly ever come to our meetings is what, for a month, I have been wondering.

The main verb does not arrive until the end of the sentence. Beginning with "Why . . . " may make the sentence slightly more difficult for an ACT reader to process, but it is definitely more interesting than this:

> *I have been wondering about something for a month. You hardly ever come to our meetings. Why?*

Loose sentences are especially effective in short, quick bursts. Their low grammatical tension makes them useful in relating technical information, in giving directions, and in convincing someone that an idea is logical. But a steady succession of loose sentences will bore a reader.

Periodic sentences, on the other hand, are the roller coasters of writing. They resemble the pattern of a mind in flux and keep a reader primed for shocks and reversals. Periodic sentences withhold the main idea until the end for maximum dramatic effect. Look at the variety this writer obtains by the use of three different kinds of periodic sentences:

> *When Al finally did come back to school, he had become so wrapped up in his own ideas that he was as unable to cope with teachers as they were unable to cope with him. Eventually, after telling his English teacher that he wasn't interested in "kindergarten poetry" and his physics teacher that "physics represent zero in relation to psychics—the real science," he was allowed to graduate on the merits of his earlier work—on the condition that he didn't come to school anymore. This, I believe, must be the first recorded honorable discharge from high school.*

Actually, the final sentence is almost a loose sentence; the only interruption is the writer's "I believe." The second sentence is the one that demands the reader's full attention. In that sentence the writer's grammatical core—that subject-verb-object relationship—is not completed until the second dash.

If you can alternate loose and periodic sentences, you may liven up a lackluster paragraph. Make your essay conform more closely to the rhythms of your thought, and you will make your sentences more intriguing to the ACT reader.

Re-verb-erate

" I t is 8–7, one out, and school will never start, rain will never come, sun will warm the back of your neck forever." With those words, former baseball commissioner A. Bartlett Giamatti charmingly described the allure of America's national pastime. Note, especially, the simple verbs he used: "will never start," "will never come," "will warm."

The best writers work in verbs. As grammarian Karen Elizabeth Gordon put it, "The verb is the heartthrob of a sentence." You would do well to pay close attention to the verbs you use, and one great place to look for exciting verbs is the sports section of your daily paper. Consider these verbs taken from the headlines of a single sports section: stifles, battles, tarnishes, turns back, dominates, shocks, spoils, skins, hangs on, benches, catches, dooms, relishes, blasts. Whew! It must have been quite a day on the gridiron.

Verbs add drama to your sentences. Without them, words would simply mill around, waiting for something exciting to happen. With them, a sentence can shake you up.

One way to check the life of your verbs is to make a count of both active and linking verbs. Baseball writer Roger Angell typically uses about eight active verbs to every one linking verb. If you can come close to that 8:1 ratio, consider yourself in good company.

If you have time, go through your essay and circle every linking verb. Then eliminate as many as possible. For example, you could turn "he has a plan to" into "he plans to" or "the team had ten losses" into "the team lost ten."

If you find an interesting verb, the rest of the sentence practically writes itself. The up and down verbs of the following sentence, for example, make for good reading:

Within the last half year, my self-esteem has plummeted as my weight has shot upward.

People often talk, but are they always speaking? Perhaps they're huffing:

"I'm not," Anthony huffs, "I was just making a comment."

Why settle for a verb like *say* when *holler*, *whisper*, and *insinuate* are available? Consider whether your sentences need to be, in Patricia O'Connor's phrase, "reverb-ed." The verb is the hardest worker in a sentence—choose yours with care.

Oops, There It Is

There is no doubt that starting a sentence with *there* puts the writer on a slippery slope. For one thing, *there* is a ghost subject, a stand-in for the real one. Writers who begin with *there* are essentially saying to the ACT reader, "The star isn't available tonight; instead, playing her role will be . . ."

For another thing, *there* doesn't come by itself. Usually, the writer follows *there* with a being verb, such as *is* or *was*. So now the reader finds a sentence without a real subject and without much of a verb either. That's a recipe for dullness. For example:

There was a sense of pride among the soldiers.

Or:

There is comfort in knowing that I helped.

A companion to *there* is *it*, which often fills the same position in a sentence, as in the following:

It was a perfect day for a picnic.

Sounds like a perfect day for a nap.

And yet, as with so much writing advice, the opposite is sometimes true. Literature is full of examples of terrific sentences that begin with *there*. For example:

"There is a tide in the affairs of men, which, taken at the flood, leads on to fortune."
—William Shakespeare

The student writer in the following passage got *it* right, too, largely thanks to parallel construction:

Stanford is a pretty good school. It's got palm trees. It's got volleyball. It's got huge libraries. It's got a particle accelerator. And it's got some Nobel laureates on the faculty. Not bad at all.

The bottom line is this: starting sentences with *there* or *it* is often a sign of a lazy writer. Such a writer has failed to make the subject the true star of the sentence and has probably failed to find anything worthwhile for the subject to do. Check your essay for *there*s and *it*s. Do you see any that could be eliminated in favor of more dynamic nouns and verbs?

But, and this is a tricky "but," sometimes starting a sentence with *there* or *it* is just right. Why? It has to do with the rhythm of your sentence. Read the sentence aloud and in context—perhaps a *there* sentence offers just the pacing you need to finish a timed essay.

A Fragment of Your Imagination

Sometimes a short sentence that gets straight to the heart of the matter can bring home a dramatic point. As a student might say, "There is no need to ramble on and on and on and on and on."

The familiar words "I love you" are a great example of getting everything you want said in three short words. This simple sentence stirs up the same emotion (or more) as would a much longer sentence.

Tom Wolfe once said that if a writer wants the reader to think something is absolutely true, the writer should express it in the shortest possible sentence. Trust me.

Notice how effectively this writer uses short sentences for dramatic effect in this story about a college student who spent a semester in South America:

> As if culture, education, and great food weren't enough, here is another approach to get you to study abroad. You could meet your husband.
>
> Señorita Amanda Miller, a Spanish major, studied in Valparaiso, Chile, last year. She studied at the Universidad Catolica de Valparaiso. "I wanted to study abroad to work on my Spanish," Miller said, "but I also wanted to do something I thought I would never do." Mission accomplished.
>
> Miller met her husband-to-be at a salsa club that she and her friends from the university attended every Thursday. Sparks flew immediately.

Each paragraph ends with a brief sentence—one of five words, one of two words, and one of three words. Those short lines give the whole passage a ring of truth, almost as if the writer were dusting her hands off and saying, "That's that." No further questions needed.

Short sentences, that is to say very short sentences, can also be used to create humor, to put a smile on the ACT reader's face. Here is the lament of a student who found himself dumped for a less savory competitor:

> *You wouldn't think it mattered that much, but the fact she cheated on me with Dave hurt even more. She went from me, a well-dressed, very nice guy who gets good grades, to Dave, who smokes and smells, barely passes classes, and has no respect for anyone. That hurts.*

For pith and power, nothing beats the simple sentence. Newspaper writers know this and bank on it, because in journalism, "You get paid by the period." And if short sentences are good, sometimes fragments are even better. Consider, for example, Muhammad Ali's comments just before a fight with George Foreman:

> *"Only last week, I murdered a rock. Injured a stone. Hospitalized a brick. I'm so mean, I make medicine sick."*

You must be thinking, That's not fair. When I write a sentence fragment, I lose points. What's the difference? Some modern grammarians call these fragments "minor sentences" because even though they're grammatically shortened, they make sense. In other words, it's OK to break the rules when you know you're breaking the rules. Of course, breaking too many rules on the ACT essay could get you penalized, so be judicious.

Tested You Will Be

magine a spaceship crash-landing in a remote jungle. The pilot climbs out of the ship and discovers a green gnome standing nearby—a gnome named, of course, Yoda.

> Yoda: *Away with your weapon! I mean you no harm. I am wondering, why are you here?*
> Luke: *I'm looking for someone.*
> Yoda: *Looking? Found someone, you have, I would say, hmm?*
> Luke: *Right.*
> Yoda: *Help you I can. Yes, mmm.*

What kind of gibberish is Yoda speaking? And more important, is it grammatically correct?

As Luke discovers, Yoda is quite astute, and in more ways than one. Yoda is speaking perfectly good English, although it is English of a rather strange sort.

We are used to sentences that follow a standard subject-verb-object order, as in *Peter Piper picked a peck of pickled peppers.* What Yoda does is simply invert this order by placing the verb or object before the subject:

Hard to see, the dark side is.

Use the force you must, young Skywalker!

These sentences aren't backward, exactly, and they actually aren't difficult to understand. But they do intrigue us because they sound so strange.

You can use this effect yourself, even if you aren't good with a light saber. In the following passage the writer creates an ironic description of her cafeteria and uses inverted word order to highlight the place's alleged cleanliness:

The environment is very pleasing as well. The staff is so avid about keeping the place spick and span that they'll just vacuum the floor as you are eating. Talk about overachievers. The silverware is also kept very clean. Only twice have my friends had a dirty fork.

Reversing standard word order does cause some English teachers to bristle. That's because it frequently leads to passive sentences, a no-no according to most guidebooks. As Strunk and White put it, for example, "The active voice is usually more direct and vigorous than the passive." Good advice. In most cases, it's a smart strategy to put the subject first.

Passive sentences typically conceal a key piece of information: the subject, or in other words, the responsible party. If you're trying to avoid blame, a passive's your game: "Mistakes were made" or "The pedestrian went under my car."

So it's best not to use passive verbs. But on occasion, it's refreshing to use inverted word order. Tennyson certainly did in his famous poem "The Charge of the Light Brigade": "All in the valley of Death/Rode the six hundred." If you're saving a surprise for the end, here's one more trick hold up your sleeve you should.

Make
Pronouns Point

"Who's on first. What's on second. I don't know's on third." These lines from a famous comic routine highlight a common writing error: ambiguous reference. In the routine Bud Abbott and his partner Lou Costello attempt to name the players on a baseball team. Abbott warns Costello that the players have odd names, but this doesn't prevent confusion.

The first baseman's name, for example, is Who. "Who is playing first?" asks Costello. "That's right," replies Abbott. "When the first baseman gets paid, who gets the money?" asks Costello. "Why not?" responds Abbott. "He earned it." And hilarity ensues.

This error plagues almost all writers from time to time, but the development of a critical awareness as you write can help reduce it to the bare minimum. Consider the following sentence:

> Garry first became acquainted with Marc one year ago when he enrolled in the lecture and laboratory sections of his molecular biology course.

Who is teaching whom? Was Garry or Marc the student? Pronouns serve as proxies for other nouns. As Patricia O'Connor explains, "Pronouns stand in when nouns don't want to hang around sounding repetitive." But a pronoun should be used only when its reference is clear. The sentence could be improved by substituting either name for *he*. For example:

Garry first became acquainted with Marc one year ago when Marc enrolled in the lecture and laboratory sections of his molecular biology course.

Identifying one of the people as a professor, *Professor Duncan* instead of *Garry*, for example, might help too.

This kind of mistake can occur just as easily with plural pronouns:

To be sure that her children saw her notes, Mother stuck them under the magnet on the refrigerator.

Pronouns are supposed to refer to the most recent noun—*notes*, in this case—but we tend to think *them* refers to people and thus are likely to conclude that Mother stuck her children to the refrigerator. This is a case of referential ambiguity; we don't know which noun *them* is replacing. An improved sentence might look like this:

To be sure her children got the message, Mother placed her notes under the magnet on the refrigerator.

A pronoun works best when it refers to a specific noun. When the writer asks the pronoun to refer to ideas, things can get murky. For instance:

*The Missouri River contained many rapids that were located in the upper portion of the river. **This** is when a large boulder is in the middle of the river and the water runs into the rock, creating a fast movement.*

Is the word *this* referring to the river, the rapids, the location of the rapids, or even the idea that the river contained some rapids? The answer is unknown, perhaps even to the writer.

Ambiguous pronoun references can also create unintended humor, as in this quote from a church bulletin:

> *Next Sunday a special collection will be taken to defray the cost of the new carpet. All those wishing to do something on the carpet should come forward and do so.*

And doing something takes on new meaning.

All the World's Offstage

Writing is ultimately about reading. Your aim as a writer is to make the ACT reader's job as easy as possible. One way to accomplish that goal is to move yourself out of the way. If you keep intruding between the reader and subject by making yourself the center of the writing universe, you're making life difficult for the reader. As kids might say when someone walks in front of the television, "You make a better door than a window."

Of course ACT readers want to know what happened to you and what you think about things. But you can convey that information without making every other word *me*, *myself*, or *I*. As best you can, try to eliminate phrases like "I think that," or "I believe," or "in my opinion." To anyone reading your essay, it will be clear that these are your thoughts, your opinions, your beliefs. The reader does not need to be continually reminded.

For example, consider this sentence:

I came to college to get a job, and this class did nothing to help me with that.

The sentence raises several questions in the reader's mind: Was the student in the right college? The right class? These questions involve the writer's credibility. To avoid all that and get the reader to the point you want to make, pull *I* and *me* out of the sentence:

This particular class will not help students prepare for a career.

Nothing's been lost and much has been gained.

Sometimes removing yourself from your writing can help you avoid blame—a good thing to remember as you write your ACT essay. Imagine you made this statement to a police officer:

> *The guy was all over the road; I had to swerve a number of times before I hit him.*

Your insurance agent might have counseled you, instead, to say:

> *The guy was swerving so much he was impossible to avoid.*

Now the burden of proof has changed hands. Consider this example from a movie review:

> *Like I said, to make a movie series and have it be good, the plot line should be fairly similar, but new characters, new problems, different settings should all be used.*

The *like I said* phrase leaves the door open for the ACT reader to dismiss the whole argument by thinking, "Well, that's just his opinion." You could achieve a much more authoritative (and believable) tone by leaving out the personal references:

> *For a movie series to be successful, the producers need to add new characters, problems, and settings while continuing a familiar plot.*

But don't fret. Even if you remove *I*, *me*, and *mine* from your writing, the ACT readers will still love you.

Gender Bender

Remember terms like *repairman, housewife,* and *Mother Nature?* How about phrases such as *act like a lady* and *man to man?* Fortunately, those words have been dumped in the dustbin of history because we have all become sensitized to sexist language.

Instead, we've learned to say (and write) *flight attendant* for *stewardess, handmade* for *manmade,* and even *fair play* for *sportsmanship.* Despite the efforts of some enthusiasts, however, we've resisted *herstory* for *history, spinster of arts degree* for *bachelor of arts degree,* and *male nurse.*

But alas, writers have discovered that it can be more difficult to eliminate sexism when it comes to pronouns. The traditional all-purpose pronoun, for instance, is male. In other words, it's technically correct to write "Each person has his own umbrella" even when each person isn't a him. Sometimes referred to as the "generic he," this pesky pronoun is routinely used when the antecedent noun is singular:

> *If a student studies hard, he will succeed on the ACT essay.*

The way to find a less gender-specific alternative has been fraught with silliness. In an effort to be inclusive, some writers have resorted to the slash as in *he/she* or *he or she*:

> *If a student studies hard, he or she will succeed on the ACT essay.*

That solution works reasonably well in a short sentence but quickly becomes ridiculous when the pronoun must be used repeatedly:

If a student studies his or her geometry and his or her social studies, he or she will likely make the honor roll.

Another popular alternative matches a plural pronoun with a singular noun:

Does each student have their book?

This choice is clearly ungrammatical. Even the best of intentions can't cover a logical mistake like that.

Some writers have decided to alternate using *he* with *she*:

The average student is worried about his grades. Ask the student to turn in her work as soon as possible.

But it's hard to remember whose turn it is, and besides, that hasn't really solved the problem. A few writers have even chosen to always use female pronouns as a sort of grammatical affirmative action. But that just replaces male sexism with female sexism.

Fortunately, there are some better choices. Here are some recommended by the National Council of Teachers of English.

1. **Drop the pronoun altogether.** Instead of "The average student is worried about his grades," use "The average student is worried about grades."
2. **Rewrite the sentence in the passive voice.** Instead of "Each student should hand in his paper promptly," use "Papers should be handed in promptly."

But most of the time, there's an even better solution. Simply make the singular noun plural. Instead of "Give the student his grade right away," use "Give the students their grades right away." Working to eliminate the sexism from your language may seem like too much political correctness, but what's wrong with being fair? It's much harder to overcome a bad impression once you've created one.

Just ask the ACT readerman.

Don't Misunderestimate the Right Place

ometimes the right word is a new word. Hundreds of words enter our language every year. For example, the Internet has brought us *interface* (to meet, as in "Let's interface"), *multitask* (to do several things at once), and *reboot* (to start over). Slang, especially teenage slang, brings us other words, such as *hottie, tight, phat,* and *for schizzle* (Snoop Dogg's version of "for sure").

New word combinations also enrich our vocabularies. Recent additions in this category include *suicide bomber, weapons of mass destruction,* and *homeland security.* Poets are famous for coining new words. For example, e. e. cummings reminded us that in spring, the world is *mudluscious* and *puddle-wonderful.*

President George W. Bush, or "Dubya" (another new word), has contributed several new words to the national vocabulary, including the oddly logical *misunderestimate.* Paul Payack, chairman of an online dictionary, said, "There are already 11,000 instances of 'misunderestimate' on the Web. The more people use words, the more likely they are to enter the language and last for generations."

Other so-called Bushisms include *embetter* (to make emotionally better—the opposite of embitter), *resignate* (as in, "They said this issue wouldn't resignate with the people"), and *foreign-handed* (as in, "I have a foreign-handed foreign policy").

So, the moral of this story is that it's occasionally OK (*OK*, by the way, is the planet's most frequently used word, no matter what language) to coin words, that is, to make them up. In fact, we do this all the time. It's one of the beauties of our language. If, for example, your group is complaining instead of brainstorming for solutions, you might write that they were *blamestorming*.

On the ACT essay, you're better off sticking to the tried and true. If you do happen upon a clever new word, however, one that just fits your essay, use it with a touch of humility and a good dose of humor. Be sure it's clear that you know the word is a bit off. Otherwise, the ACT rater may just make your new term *misappear*.

Pound the Concrete

Word choice matters, not only on the ACT but for the rest of your life. In fact, choosing the right word on a résumé can make the difference in getting the job you want. Your future employer is looking for the most qualified person to hire. You must rely on words to explain why you are that person. If you select words that are almost right, then you may find yourself almost hired. As Mark Twain once explained, "The difference between the right word and the almost right word is the difference between lightning and lightning bug."

The key is not to generalize in your writing but to use concrete details. General is boring. It asks the reader to stop reading and guess what you mean. Consider the following examples:

general: *worker*   concrete: *assistant manager*
general: *restaurant*   concrete: *International House of*
                                          Pancakes
general: *food*   concrete: *strawberry waffles*

Clearly, specific nouns (*salad bar*, *apron*, *Mavis*) provide a more detailed picture for the reader. Simply writing that you had a job at a restaurant is vague and uninteresting. You must supply the missing information if you want your writing to be memorable. And this is true in everything you write—your ACT essay, for example.

Comedian Bill Cosby took Shakespeare's famous "Seven Ages of Man" passage and updated it. You'll note that Cosby, too, uses concrete details to make his writing memorable.

The seven ages of man have become preschool, Pepsi generation, baby boomer, midlifer, empty nester, senior citizen, and organ donor.

If you want to get your prose up and running, keep your abstraction detector in good working order as you write. Be alert for those fuzzy, general, abstract subjects that seem to come to mind when you start a sentence. Suppose, for example, you wanted to analyze movie idol Johnny Depp. The first sentence you think of turns out like this:

His ability to absorb himself completely in his roles truly gives an example of pure talent in acting.

Abstract nouns such as *ability*, *example*, and *talent* make the whole sentence vague and almost meaningless. What if you had used vivid, specific nouns instead, like this:

Depp wears thick eyeliner, gold teeth, and matted, nasty hair to bring his character, pirate Jack Sparrow, to life.

Those concrete, specific nouns—*eyeliner*, *teeth*, and *hair*—anchor this sentence in reality and make reading the sentence fun. Of course, if you had Johnny Depp's dimples, you might be reading a Hollywood script right now instead of this book.

Gobble Gobbledygook

ood writers communicate in lean, clean language. They don't waste the ACT reader's time with superfluous words. Just as athletes need strong muscles and low body fat to move quickly and avoid tiring, writers need strong verbs and low writing fat (unneeded words) to set a brisk pace and avoid exhausting the reader.

The following is a flabby memo sent to President Franklin Roosevelt for his approval during World War II:

In the unlikely event of an attack by an invader of a foreign nature, such preparation shall be made as will completely obscure all Federal buildings and non-Federal buildings occupied by the Federal government during an air raid for any period of time from visibility by reason of internal or external illumination.

Here's how Roosevelt trimmed that memo:

If there's an air raid, put something across the windows and turn off the outside lights in buildings where we have to keep the work going.

The memo sent to Roosevelt was couched in gobbledygook—wordy, redundant, unnecessarily complex writing—the antithesis of clear, direct writing. Those who write gobbledygook care more about impressing than communicating.

While such writing might impress those afflicted with Academic Dysfunctional Communication Syndrome, it is a bane to others. Look carefully at your writing to see if every word is carrying its weight. How many words, for example, are really needed in the following sentence? "The Lewis and Clark expedition was thought up by the president of the United States of America; at that time it was Thomas Jefferson." Would "The Lewis and Clark expedition was conceived by President Thomas Jefferson" get the job done just as well?

To be technical, don't let adjectives and adverbs weaken your message. Be on the lookout for useless adjectives, as in these examples, with corrections in parentheses: *past history* (*history*), *personal opinion* (*opinion*), *baby kitten* (*kitten*), and *blue in color* (*blue*).

In the same way, watch for places where you can use a strong verb to replace a weak adverb. Here are some examples:

Instead of	*He **ran quickly** down the field.*
Prefer	*He **sped** down the field.*
Instead of	*The cat **suddenly jumped** on the mouse.*
Prefer	*The cat **pounced** on the mouse.*

Or: *The student sped down the hallway and pounced on the ACT.* You get the idea.

Some Words Are Very, Very Bad

t seems odd, doesn't it? Your mother probably told you that certain words should *never* be used in polite company. You know the words. Yes, *those* words. And yet there are certain words that we commonly use when we talk but should never use in print. How can that be?

These unmentionable words are vague qualifiers, words such as *really, very, truly, basically,* and *totally.* They are valuable in speech because they allow us to buy a little breathing time—we can get by with the less-than-precise word until we have time to think of what we mean to say exactly.

But when we write, we can be more selective. When we use fewer qualifiers, our sentences become tighter, clearer, and more concrete. Thus, *very happy,* or worse, *very, very happy* becomes *joyful.*

For example, notice the qualifiers this writer uses in a description of a wedding reception:

The food was very good and tasty. It was a buffet, which included fruit, roast beef, baked potatoes, turkey, and rolls. The turkey and potatoes were a little cold, but overall it was very good. The dance was very fun, and a lot of good songs were played. The dance floor was filled with many people having fun and dancing like fools. Overall, the whole experience was very elegant. The wedding was a little longer than usual but was very beautiful. The dinner and dance were also held at a very nice place with great food and a fun dance.

You might think this example is silly, but consider whether vague qualifiers such as *very* sneak into your prose without your ever noticing. Remove the qualifiers, sharpen a few observations, and you might get this:

> *The wedding reception featured a tasty buffet with fruit, roast beef, baked potatoes, turkey, and rolls, though some of the food was cold. After dinner, the dance floor began to fill with people making fools of themselves—an especially amusing sight because everything else about the event was elegant. The wedding may have taken longer than usual, but the location, the buffet dinner, and the dance all made for an enjoyable evening.*

Is this a universal rule, something true in every case? No. In the hands of great writers, anything is possible. All the rules go out the window. Here Stephen King uses *really* in a most effective way:

> *Of course movies matter. But, you might ask, do movies **really** matter? Do they matter the way great books do, or great plays like* King Lear? . . . *My answer is you bet your sweet round fanny.*

Still, if you can strip the qualifiers from your sentences most of the time, you'll get your writing down to where the rubber hits the road. Then you can let nouns and verbs do the heavy lifting as in this student evaluation: "This class made me laugh, sometimes cry, dry my eyes to try and try, question reality, laugh at authority, scoff at accepted truths, and made me long to teach poetry."

And I Said What I Meant

The main object of prose writing is the transfer of meaning from writer to reader—clearly, and in the fewest words possible. Striving to write efficiently can help you cope with the time constraints posed by the ACT essay.

Simple and direct language, and generally short sentences and paragraphs, make the ACT reader's job easier. Don't force readers to use their mental energy wrestling with unnecessarily difficult or cloudy writing. Let them save that energy for complex ideas.

Writing that is choked with polysyllabic words, for example, can make hard reading. Have you ever read a product manual, article, or textbook that was so foggy that you had to work just to tease the meaning from one paragraph? Who hasn't, right?

But wait, you say, that was a complex subject, and a complex subject needs complex language. Wrong. Just because you're dealing with a complicated subject doesn't mean your language has to be.

W. Somerset Maugham put it this way:

I have never had much patience with the writers who claim from the reader an effort to understand their meaning. You have only to go to the great philosophers to see that it is possible to express with lucidity the most subtle reflections. You may find it difficult to understand the thought of Hume, and if you have no philosophical training, its implications will doubtless escape you; but no one with any education at all can fail to understand exactly what the meaning of each sentence is.

That said, it's also true that complex words and sentences are needed in good writing, but the point is to find the right balance between high-octane writing (rich, polysyllabic words and phrases) and more economical, utilitarian prose (single-syllable words).

Monitor your writing. Select 100 consecutive words from a practice essay and divide by the number of sentences. The result will give you your average sentence length. Studies have shown that an average of 16 or 17 words fits most readers' comfort level.

It takes skill and an ordered mind to express complex ideas in simple language. Remember Albert Einstein's $E = mc^2$? The more complex the idea, the greater the need to keep your language simple.

Cut the Clutter

eyewitness at the scene

10:00 A.M. *in the morning*

two twins

If you can't see an easy way to shorten those phrases without losing the meaning, you may be guilty of repetitiveness in your writing. It's an easy trap for all of us.

The fact is, though, good writing is efficient. An ethical writer shouldn't ask any more of the ACT reader's time than is strictly necessary. And when you repeat yourself, you're asking more from the reader than you're entitled to. So the challenge is to be on guard lest redundancies slip into your sentences unnoticed.

One of the easiest ways to be redundant is to add a useless preposition at the end of a phrase: *canceled **out**, went **away**, shouted **out**, send **in**, continue **on**.* The prepositions *up* and *down* are especially dangerous—*open **up**, wrote **down**, fell **down**, divided **up***, and so on.

Another form of repetition occurs when a writer puts a synonym on either side of *and*—for example, *safe and sound, plain and simple, each and every.* We also use two words where one would get the job done. See if you can reduce each of the following by one or two words:

absolutely necessary
advance planning
ask the question

at the present time
basic fundamentals
close proximity
other alternatives
refer back
both of them
in the year 2005
first of all

Sometimes you can think of a different word to replace a string of words:

on one occasion . . . . .once
a small number of . . . . .a few
went on to say . . . . .continued
all of a sudden . . . . .suddenly
a large number of . . . . .many
was able to make his escape . . . .escaped

With a little work and some careful editing, you can do your part to slim down American prose. Here's how. Take this passage of thirty-six words:

> *Weight loss is a constant battle in which it seems there is no end. A friend of mine recently told me that she used to have an eating disorder and continues to struggle with it currently.*

And cut it in half:

> *Weight loss is a constant battle. A friend recently told me she is still struggling with an eating disorder.*

Sometimes a loss is a gain.

An Element of Stylin'

Style in writing refers to the voice readers hear speaking to them between the lines. Voice, as you might guess, implies personality. What kind of person does your ACT reader think you are? How does the reader form that impression?

When a writer selects a style, however unconsciously, and thus presents a personality to a reader, in Walker Gibson's words, he or she "chooses certain words and not others, and prefers certain arrangements of words to other possible arrangements." Every choice you make is significant to style.

Let's take a look at three familiar styles in modern American prose—Tough Talk, Sweet Talk, and Stuffy Talk. The way we write at any given moment can be a form of one of these three basic styles, or perhaps a combination.

Tough Talkers are mainly concerned with themselves—their style is I-talk. Sweet Talkers go out of their way to be nice to us—their style is you-talk. Stuffy Talkers express no concern for themselves or their reader—their style is it-talk. Tough Talkers tend to use a lot of one-syllable words, while Stuffy Talkers prefer two- or three-syllable words. Sweet Talkers are somewhere in between.

Here's an example of Tough Talk by one of the toughest talkers of all time, Ernest Hemingway:

In the late summer of that year we lived in a house in a village that looked across the river and the plain to the mountains. In the bed of the river there were pebbles and boulders, dry and white in the sun, and the water was clear and swiftly moving and blue in the channels.

Here's some Sweet Talk from the world of advertising:

> *You may have tried Kraft Dinners before and been delighted at how quick and easy they are—and how unusually good. Well, wait till you taste these new Dinners from Kraft. They're complete, the finest of their kind, made with all the best Kraft ingredients.*

And a little Stuffy Talk from government bureaucrats:

> *In previous studies the use of tobacco, especially cigarette smoking, has been causally linked to several diseases. These widely reported findings, which have been the cause of much public concern over the past decade, have been accepted in many countries by official health agencies, medical associations, and voluntary health organizations.*

To determine your own style, take a short chunk of your writing and count the words. If three-fourths (75 percent) or more of the words you use are one-syllable words, you're a Tough Talker. Sweet Talkers use about two-thirds and Stuffy Talkers about half. Now count the number of words with more than two syllables. If the percentage is low (about 5 percent), you're a Tough Talker. Stuffy Talkers use about 25 percent. As you might guess, the Tough Talker mainly writes in first person (*I, me, mine*), the Sweet Talker in second person (*you, your*), and the Stuffy Talker in third person (*he, she, they*).

The goal is to adjust your style for the particular writing task you face. If you're writing an e-mail message to a friend, Tough Talk works just fine. If you're trying to convince Mom or Dad to pay for your car insurance, try Sweet Talk. If you're writing a research paper on T. S. Eliot, Stuffy Talk might be the best choice. On the ACT essay, a combination of Tough and Stuffy is probably best. Save the Sweet Talk for those warm, romantic moments *after* the test.

The Rolling Tones in Concert

Tone might be described as the emotional quality a writer brings to the work. We expect a dark painting to be somber, perhaps even mysterious. Words can command the same effect: no one would mistake Poe's macabre tone in a poem or story.

The following example, written as a description of a Rolling Stones concert, certainly conveys an emotional tone:

> *Being July Fourth, it was mighty hot, and believe me everyone dressed for the occasion. There was an influx of hot pants, halter tops, one-size-fits-all bras, and, last but not least, one birthday suit that was soon to have the candles blown out.*

This writer reveals a sense of excitement, but just exactly what caused that excitement is hard to know. This is tone in search of meaning.

By contrast, sometimes language is almost atonal, that is, without any emotional coloring at all. The various publications of the government are examples of the purest objective writing. In those official reports, emotional connotations are played down as much as possible.

The following example was written not by a government bureaucrat but by a student who was probably trying too hard to please. Her writing might be termed "overcontrolled." The descriptions are precise, but they have the effect of dehumanizing her characters.

> *The presence of older people at Northern Virginia Community College is a tremendous asset to the educational opportunities it offers. Their influence upon the people around them is obvious. They are a stabilizing force in a changing community, and they have the capacity to slow us down, to make us think. We respect them, and we learn from their vast sources of experience. Perhaps most important, these special individuals lend a certain degree of reality to classroom situations.*

This kind of writing sounds like something a machine might have composed. A better balance between these two extremes—all emotion and no emotion—is needed.

One way a writer can prove an ability to control a word's emotional impact as well as its literal meaning is by using irony. In the following example, a writer proposes a change that will revolutionize human life, but his tone resembles that of a city council ordinance.

> *While I am not advocating complete removal of the law of gravity (Lord knows where we would be without it), there is no doubt in my mind that a great majority of the population would benefit from the elimination of this "Mickey Mouse" law. Under my plan, the force of gravity would be minimized in areas where it has the greatest detrimental effect; i.e., near the ground or in sections of water beneath famous bridges such as the Brooklyn or Golden Gate bridges.*

The moral of this story is that a writer should be sensitive to the emotional nuances of words. Now, where's Mick Jagger when we need satisfaction?

Seeing with Your Ears

"A good word is worth a thousand pictures," said Eric Sevareid, a longtime CBS radio and television correspondent. Sevareid understood the power of words to influence our thinking. When we hear words on the radio—without the benefit of seeing what is described—we create the pictures in our minds. "TV gives everyone a picture," Peggy Noonan, speechwriter for President Ronald Reagan, said, "but radio gives birth to a million pictures in a million minds."

Now you may never become a presidential speechwriter, but you do want the ACT reader to remember what you say and to take your ideas seriously. To make those ideas memorable, put a picture in the reader's mind.

Take Shakespeare, for example. We can't forget these words: "Friends, Romans, countrymen, lend me your ears." As comic Bob Newhart wondered, would anyone have paid attention to, "Listen up, folks. I've got something I want to tell you."

One way to give your readers some mental images is to use similes or metaphors. These eccentric and sometimes outrageous comparisons join two unlike things. For example:

I felt as if I were drowning in homework.

Or:

Then he kissed her, like a butterfly kisses the windshield of a Porsche on the autobahn.

A simile uses the words *like* or *as* to help make the comparison, as in the following examples:

She yelled at us like a cheetah tearing into flesh.

Or:

Words rolled through the air from my teacher's mouth like a tumbleweed rolling across the desert of my brain.

It's not hard to imagine a wild animal eating or a tumbleweed blowing across a desert. Mental images similar to these can pop into the head of the reader, who then thinks, "OK, yeah, now I know what you're talking about."

Metaphors, on the other hand, are direct comparisons and need no other help: "I feel the chains of stress and monotony weighing down on my weary spirit." By using two things that are seemingly unrelated (stress and chains), the writer gives us a sense of how drastic or serious the situation might be. Chains, as we know, are heavy and tiresome; by applying them to stress, we get a sense of what turmoil the narrator is going through.

Metaphors are a challenge because they must be original, created expressly for a particular time and place. A metaphor lasts about as long as egg salad left out on the counter—use it while it's fresh and then forget about it. Once-clever metaphors quickly become worn out and empty.

So, when you're looking to create a memorable image, turn to your old friends simile and metaphor. After all, you are the artist with the word palette.

Make Your Essay Count

The three bears. The three little pigs. Cinderella and her two ugly stepsisters. Three is clearly the magic number when it comes to storytelling. Three is somehow satisfying: not too many, not too few, just right.

Speechwriters often search for three examples of whatever point they wish to make. The first example causes the listener to think, "Oh, I suppose." The second example causes the listener to think, "Well, that seems right." The third example, the clincher, is the one that causes the listener to think, "Why, yes, that must be it." The number three just seems to have an aura of invincibility.

But other numbers have value for writers too. Take one, for example, the "loneliest number" as the rock band Three Dog Night sang. The number one commits the writer to a single thought: "Make mine a latte." In this simple sentence, as writing coach Roy Peter Clark notes, the writer declares a single defining characteristic. The reader must focus on that and nothing else. For example:

Just do it.

I have a dream.

I have a headache.

The number two has its own special talents. Use it, for example, to complicate issues. "Make mine a latte with a shot of espresso." Here the writer doesn't ask us to make a choice; instead, the writer makes us hold two possibilities in our minds at the same time. For example:

Green eggs and ham

Grits and gravy

Donald Trump and "You're fired"

Sentences with two items ask the reader to balance, to compare and contrast. They place us on the twin horns of a dilemma.

That brings us back to three. The number three enables us to surround a subject, to triangulate, as it were. "Make mine a latte with a shot of espresso and add some whipped cream on top." Now we see the subject in a well-rounded way. In our culture, three seems to give us a sense of the whole. For example:

Beginning, middle, and end

Of the people, by the people, for the people

Larry, Moe, and Curly

At the end of his famous passage on the nature of love in the Book of Corinthians, Paul writes, "For now, faith, hope, and love abide, these three." Could he have said it any better?

So, writing is as easy as one, two, three, right? Well, what about four? Five? Six? Once the writer goes beyond three, the sky's the limit. "Make that a double latte with a shot of espresso, whipped cream, a whisper of cinnamon, and a cocoa bean on the side."

What do more examples add to a sentence—a list, a roster, an inventory? They provide a powerful sense of detail. "The Lewis and Clark expedition encountered the Omaha, Ponca, Arikara, Mandan, Hidatsa, Shoshone, Nez Percé, Clatsop, and Walla Walla tribes, to name a few."

As for the ACT essay, think six. More coffee, anyone?

Too Close to Call

The semicolon is a much-neglected beast. A. P. Rossiter, one of the finest Shakespearean commentators of his generation, was a champion of the semicolon; he rarely let a paragraph go by without finding some reason to slip one in. But many writers, and particularly students, seem to use it with great reluctance. And yet the semicolon offers interesting possibilities to bring variety and elegance to your writing.

The semicolon is useful when two independent thoughts belong together in one sentence. The semicolon connects independent elements; that is, it joins two groups of words that could each stand alone but somehow have something important in common.

With the semicolon, what you see is what you get: it acts like a period and a comma fused. It can be distinguished from its close relative, the colon, by this principle of independence—the words that follow a colon do not need to be able to stand alone. Compare these two sentences:

1. He liked all kinds of vegetables: peas, beans, collards, and potatoes.
2. He liked all kinds of vegetables; he particularly liked peas, beans, collards, and potatoes.

The semicolon can also be used to separate items in a series when those items already use commas, as, for example, in a list of cities:

Pierre, South Dakota; Bismarck, North Dakota; and Ames, Iowa

Or a sentence like this:

From a balcony, one can not only hear the gossip about Signora Benetti's daughter, but one can see Anna industriously setting the dinner table for her mamma; one can hear Ricardo's fingers gently meandering over the strings of his guitar; and one can smell the pasta and sauce which each good Italian mamma in the neighborhood is preparing for dinner.

But this is easy. What really requires the writer's delicacy is to create a sentence with a fragile balance between two separate thoughts that seem to have one common purpose:

Fletcher Christian's men, after taking over the Bounty, seemingly disappeared from the face of the earth; nearly twenty years were to pass before their hiding place was found.

Some people say that semicolons are most frequently used in formal language, that professors are fond of them because they make sentences long—and long sentences appear to be more intellectually rigorous. But they work for all of us.

If you find yourself using *and* too often or notice that you've written too many short, choppy sentences, give the semicolon a try. It won't just make your sentences better; it will make them more interesting too—especially to a beleaguered ACT reader.

Add Some Body Language

The showman Victor Borge had a comic routine in which he gave
sounds to punctuation. A comma, said Borge, sounds like a
squiggle looks, and he would make a noise roughly equivalent
to the sound of a rag cleaning a glass window. A period sounded
like the German word for period, *punkt*. And of course, the semicolon was a combination of those two sounds. Borge's colon was a
double punkt, and his dash was a vocal rendition of the sound
Zorro's sword used to make. Once Borge had demonstrated the
sound of each of these marks, he would use them as he read poetry
aloud to the audience.

Borge's routine reminds us that the writer makes music in the
mind's ear. In particular, two punctuation marks—the dash and
the colon—can provide the rhythm of jazz to writing.

For example, Borge's dash (the sword of Zorro) was swift—the
dash speeds up a sentence. It signifies an immediate association in
the writer's mind between one thing and another and propels the
ACT reader furiously from one thought to the next.

Use the dash to indicate a sudden change in tone. For example:

*On the mosquito's sides had been two flattened sacs, and from
them she now pulled out—wings!*

Use the dash when you want to add something by shouting:

*The next day Mrs. Blakewell—what a pest she is!—
complained to Dad about the noise we had made.*

And the dash can be used at the end of a sentence when the writer wishes to make an abrupt point or summary:

We had only one choice—escape.

Meanwhile, let's not forget another useful mark: the colon. Remember that Borge's colon was a double period and hence almost a double stop. It gives the writer a way to tell the reader to hit the brakes but then to continue, sort of like a flashing red light. The colon is helpful for introducing a list:

For a first date, you have a few options: you can go out to eat, you can go to a movie, or you can go to someone's house and watch TV.

Or dramatizing a leap in thought:

Cancer: one of life's biggest threats.

The colon performs many of the same functions as the dash but at a more leisurely pace. When pondering which to use, consider whether your reader is dashing out the door for work or idling in an easy chair, watching the snow fall outside the window.

And if you really want to make an impact, add a few italics, as in this example from Betsy Haynes's teen romance *The Truth About Taffy Sinclair*:

Suddenly I saw something that made my heart stop. Jana Morgan and her friends were standing in a tight little cluster looking at something that Jana was holding. They were giggling and talking excitedly. I knew without looking. They had found the last thing in the world I wanted them to see—*my secret, personal diary!*

Ah yes, the truth and Taffy are sometimes stretched.

Parenthetically Speaking

Most of the pens and pencils I own don't seem to have a volume control. In fact, none of them do. And yet all of them are capable of helping to raise or lower a writer's voice.

You can use parentheses when you want to whisper. In this sentence, for example, "The teacher told me I had a 1.6 GPA (whatever GPA means)," the writer didn't want to announce his or her ignorance to the whole world—at least not very loudly.

Parentheses can be used to add a comment in the middle of a sentence. "One of my idiot friends (idiot being an understatement) did the dumbest thing today." Parentheses are also used to enclose comments directed straight at the reader: "How much is $40 thousand worth to Martha Stewart? That amount of money works out to roughly .006 percent of her net worth (nothing to lose sleep over)."

Parentheses set off material that the author does not consider necessary to understand the basic meaning of the sentence. A remark tucked inside a pair of parentheses looks as if the writer could have dropped it altogether (which is why it was hidden inside parentheses). Sometimes when students read passages aloud, they skip over anything inside parentheses, instinctively recognizing the nonessential.

But parentheses also allow a writer to develop a double voice. They enable the writer to comment on the action, much like a stage manager explaining a play to the audience. Those comments can be ironic:

Class time is (unfortunately) used to maximum potential.

Or humorous:

> *"The Simpsons" remains one of the best programs on television with its priceless Homerisms ("We love queens, be they homecoming or dairy") combined with sight gags and celebrity cameos.*

Or even allow a dog to think:

> *Then he stroked my nose (I tell you, he really does love me!), brushed my fur, adjusted my leash, and pushed me out the door.*

By the way, did you notice the exclamation point? Exclamation points create a powerful contrast to parentheses because they indicate strong emotion, either positive or negative: "Stop, you can't go in there!" or "Henry, I love you!"

When you state something with emotion, you can't really do much to make the reader feel that emotion. Are you going to write it in big bold letters? No. Are you going to underline it? No. That's where exclamation points come in.

Check out how exclamation points affect the way you interpret these sentences:

> *"Wait, don't touch that button!"* (You're not asking people politely; you're trying to scare the bejesus out of them.)

> *"Oh Romeo, I love you so much!"* (This isn't a crush in junior high; this is deep down love.)

But use both parentheses and exclamation points sparingly in your ACT essay. They can give the readers a feeling that you are standing over their shoulders and either whispering or shouting in their ears. That can be fun for a while—a short while.

The Pudding Is in the Proof

Imagine that you have just five minutes to finish your ACT essay. You frantically check your progress. Whoops. You haven't thought of a conclusion yet, and you wanted to go back and fix the first sentence. Yikes.

But have you proofread? "Proofread? Yeah, right," you say to yourself. "I barely have time to write another sentence. Why proofread anyway; that's the teacher's job."

Actually, proofreading is an essential step in the writing process. The essay is not complete when you stop writing. Simple spelling errors, such as those that a click on the spell-check button would fix, show the ACT reader that you don't sincerely care about your essay.

Here are a few pointers for proofreading. After you finish your essay, take a moment's break (I know, you'll have to plan ahead). Read once through to check the sense. Even though the sentences are grammatically correct and none of the words are misspelled, something might still be wrong:

Loida Whitson called her sister, Dorcas, in the Philippines on Dorcas's thirtieth birthday. She talked to everyone there.
(That might have been quite a phone bill!)

He walked across the room and kissed her where she sat. (I'll bet she was surprised!)

Use common sense, too. Look for places where the meaning could be misconstrued, such as in these church bulletin bloopers:

Our next song is "Angels We Have Heard Get High."

Remember in prayer the many who are sick of our church and community.

Weight Watchers will meet at 7:00 P.M. Please use large double door at the side entrance.

Be on the lookout, too, for words that are slightly askew:

When Christopher Columbus and his European comrades first set foot on North American soil in 1492, it did not take long for them to run into the Native Americans who inhibited the land. (I wonder how the Native Americans lost their inhibitions?)

Finally, try reading your paper aloud (very quietly, of course). Anything that makes you cringe when you hear it needs rewriting.

Proofreading is that little bit of extra time and effort you put into your essay that will take it from ordinary to extraordinary—the breast paper you can write!

Things Are Looking Up

You can't use a dictionary on the ACT essay, but you can use one every other time you write. And you should. A dictionary is a writer's single greatest resource. A thesaurus, stylebook, or writing guide may be helpful at times, but they can never replace the good old dictionary.

Dictionaries supply a writer with a great wealth of material: they provide a word's most common meaning, together with examples of its use; secondary meanings; and some indication of the word's origin—useful information when questions of tone arise. Generally, words of Latin origin are longer and blandly neutral; words of Anglo-Saxon origin are frequently shorter and more vivid. Special dictionaries such as the *Oxford English Dictionary* provide other information including a history of the word's meaning (which can change from age to age).

Writers who have the slightest hesitation about the precise meaning of a word should consult a dictionary. That way, they can avoid problems such as those in the following humorous examples from some course evaluations:

> *This class is fun and inciteful.* (There must have been some heated discussions!)

> *The class has stretched my limitations.* (One of those limitations is writing, apparently.)

It's a challenge to read some of the more deviant works. (Not to mention diverse or offbeat.)

A dictionary can also help you avoid trouble like this:

He lets me think anteliticly about the books I am reading. (Let's analyze that.)

My only quam in this class . . . (I wonder whether a quam tastes anything like a clam.)

A dictionary can even help you know whether a word can be used as an adverb:

I have upmost enjoyed this class and having you as a professor.

As a verb:

She listens to our views and inputs her own as well.

Or as an adjective:

She gives clear explanations of terms and if the students are confused, she makes it further clear.

These days the best modern dictionaries even have pictures. Be sure that you have this essential reference work close at hand whenever you sit down to practice writing your ACT essay.

TEST
STRATEGIES

"*My personal theory is that it has to do with how much money you send them in the mail. I think the amounts they tell you to send are actually just suggested minimum donations—if you get my drift.*"
—columnist Dave Barry

D espite Barry's cynical theory that standardized tests are for sale, you still have a better chance of buying love or a member of Congress. So let's barter. You study the strategies, you get a higher score.

Have a Plan B

"One stupid test and I'm roadkill on the highway of natural selection. Do you realize my entire future is nothing more than a barren expanse of minimum wage jobs and reality TV? All leading to my eventual extinction."
—Warren Cheswick, "Ed"

On one episode of the television show "Ed," high school student Warren Cheswick bemoans his fate after learning of a low score on a standardized test. Fortunately, Cheswick has a plan B. The plan, however, is not to study harder and retake the test. Cheswick decides, instead, to give up the idea of going to college altogether. Cheswick's plan B is to immediately start his career as a talk show host on public-access television. Dare to dream, his mantra.

You are not a character on a television show. Granted, the "Tonight Show" may be in your future, but not tonight while you're preparing for an essay question. What happens if that question makes no sense to you? Or if you can't think of anything substantive to say?

It's not how much you know that counts but how well you use what you do know.

Consider the following suggestions.

I. Practice on the Nearly Impossible

In J. D. Salinger's *The Catcher in the Rye*, the central character, Holden Caulfield, flunks history. His teacher, Mr. Spencer, informs

Holden that he knew "absolutely nothing." Then Spencer reads Holden's essay exam aloud and forces him to listen.

The Egyptians were an ancient race of Caucasians residing in one of the northern sections of Africa. The latter as we all know is the largest continent in the Eastern Hemisphere. . . .

And so on. You are more fortunate than Holden. You don't have to know any facts about the Egyptians—or much else for that matter. The ACT essay question allows you to merely apply what you already know. The key is to make a meaningful connection between what is asked and what you know. Remember: *works of literature speak to each other.*

Suppose you were given the following essay topic.

Consider carefully the excerpt and the assignment below it. Then plan and write an essay that explains your ideas as persuasively as possible. Keep in mind that the support you provide—both reasons and examples—will help make your view convincing to the reader.

In Mark Twain's book *The Adventures of Huckleberry Finn*, Huck becomes more than a casual rebel against responsibility. His destiny is to learn much about what it means to be a human being. On his journey down the Mississippi, Huck meets up at one point with two ne'er-do-wells: the king and the duke. The duke refers to the people who live along the river with disdain.

". . . these Arkansaw lunkheads couldn't come up to Shakespeare; what they wanted was low comedy—and maybe something ruther worse than low comedy, he reckoned. He said he could size their style."

Assignment: What is your view on the differences that separate people? In an essay, support your position using an example (or examples) from literature, the arts, history, current events, politics, science and technology, or your experience or observations.

Now suppose you haven't read *The Adventures of Huckleberry Finn* (if so, shame on you). You are limited, therefore, to the insights you can glean from the passage quoted. Even if you are unaware that Huck is one of the good bad boys of American literature, you can infer from the passage that Twain favored him over the people of Arkansas. Is Twain's book titled *The Adventures of the Arkansaw Lunkheads?* And you are told in the blurb that the king and the duke are "ne'er-do-wells."

So your plan B becomes to flesh out the essay by applying what you have been studying recently. Let's say that your English class just finished discussing "anyone lived in a pretty how town" by e. e. cummings. At first thought, you might assume Huck and "anyone" had little in common. Don't give up so easily. Study the quoted passage again.

In cummings's poem, the "lunkheads" are the "someones" and "everyones" in life who act dutifully without joy or pleasure. Not really alive, they remain unchanged while "anyone" blossoms. The tragedy, you learn in the cummings poem, is the fate of the children. Raised by the "someones" and "everyones" of the world, these children lose their capacity to grow, in all senses of the word. Huck, you could argue, is "anyone"—a homeless waif who finds his way despite the people who surround him—the people who are already "dying," even as we first encounter them.

Other works of literature will work as well. In Athol Fugard's play *"Master Harold" . . . and the Boys*, the character Sam describes the collisions that take place between people. Using ballroom dancing as a metaphor, Sam explains how easily we are bruised by our differences—how people get hurt by all the bumping. That, as you might suspect, is part of what Huck learns about the nature of human beings.

And don't forget that you can write about your own experiences. Your journey through high school, like Huck's trip down the Mississippi, is a quest for self-knowledge. You, too, have learned much about what separates people. How accepting of a person's differences is your average clique in high school? *Go team!*

Now it's your turn. Try preparing for the ACT by answering some essay questions that are far more difficult than those questions likely to be asked by the test makers. You and a friend should make up practice essay questions for each other. Evaluate each other's completed essays. Discuss. Rethink.

2. Add to Your Tool Chest

Terry Deibel, a National War College strategist, warns, "If the only tool you've got is a hammer, every problem looks like a nail."

Even the most intransigent of desk-perados will benefit from studying the principles, strategies, and practice essays in this book. You need these tools to better prepare for any contingency.

You should also read more. Read the editorial page of a national newspaper. Contemporary poetry. Collections of short stories. Your homework. Feed your brain. Anything and everything. Dr. Tom Fischgrund's study of students who earned perfect SAT scores found that those students read nearly twice as much for school as average academic achievers. He concluded, though, that it really didn't matter much *what* was read. The key was to read a lot. Fischgrund was researching SAT results, but the implications are compelling for the ACT as well.

Keep in mind that every book you read becomes a part of you. And you want a committee of writers in your head to serve as editors for your writing. Someone on that committee should be the voice in your head screaming at you when you construct a poorly worded sentence. Another someone should whisper sweet nothings when you occasionally make sense. Collectively, these writers invited into your thinking keep your tools sharpened and at their ready.

3. Seek Sense and Sensibility

Broaden the sphere of people that influence your thinking. Include folks other than the celebrity of the moment or the popular politician. The goal here is to develop an artistic sensibility. Biographer Eric Lax wrote that Woody Allen combines "the cadences of Bob Hope, the language of S. J. Perelman, the style of George Lewis, the outlook of Mort Sahl, the obsessions of Ingmar Bergman, the zaniness of the Marx Brothers, the soulfulness of Buster Keaton, the existential dilemma of Jean-Paul Sartre, the exaggerated exoticness of Federico Fellini . . . to produce a unique sensibility."

Of course, you won't have the same influences as Allen. Nor should you. After all, Allen once admitted that he was obsessed by the fact that his mother genuinely resembled Groucho Marx. But the likelihood of writer's block greatly decreases if you welcome creative people into your neighbor-head.

4. Accept That Life Is Not Always Fair

The *Albuquerque Journal* cites this case of health care contingency planning: Surgeons cut a hole in a man's head to relieve swelling after an accident. The hospital's finance office then refused to schedule a follow-up procedure to replace the piece of skull because it was no longer an emergency.

The man did have a plan B. According to the surgeons, "The man wore a baseball cap to protect his brain until the hospital finally agreed to do the procedure."

Now don't rush out and buy a baseball cap, but do protect your brain. Bureaucracies (can you say the folks with ACT?) create nightmares for individuals like you. That's what they do. Accept that.

When you first heard, "It's not your aptitude but your attitude," you may have bitten your lip. Unclench. Cynicism don't feed the bulldog.

To defend his plan B, Cheswick clings to the fact that news anchor Peter Jennings dropped out of high school. The truth is, for most students, dropping out is the anchor.

Tell Your Truth

At age forty-two, Gilda Radner lost her battle with ovarian cancer. One of the original cast members of "Saturday Night Live," Radner was the sweetheart of Saturday nights. Her characters—the brash Roseanne Roseannadanna, the nerdy Lisa Loopner, and the misinformed Emily Litella—are part of her legacy. Radner was warm, big-hearted, courageous, and real—all qualities that you should aspire to in your writing.

Shortly before her death, she wrote a personal account of her struggle with cancer. She told the truth with the same courage she brought to performing. Radner was fearless: from shoving beans up her nose to hurling herself against a wall with rib cage–breaking force. Alan Zweibel, an "SNL" writer who published the memoir *Bunny Bunny* about their fourteen-year friendship, said, "She was accessible. She wasn't overly pretty. . . . It was just someone laying themselves out there saying, 'This is me. Like me. This is me. I'm gonna make you laugh now,' like a kid would."

In your ACT essay, you have to put yourself out there. Be unafraid. Tell the truth. As Radner's character Roseanne Roseannadanna would remind us, "It's always something." Now search your memory for the "somethings" of your life. Here are two suggestions:

1. Recycle Your Best "Somethings"

What makes a "something" into something good? Truth is the first requirement for good writing. Composer George Gershwin was once asked how long it took him to write *Rhapsody in Blue*. He replied, "All my life." Like Gershwin, your truth is shaped by every experience you've ever had. It's the way you tell what happened, though, that matters. A common experience can be described in language that makes it memorable.

Author Wallace Stegner calls this writing the "dramatization of belief." In her introduction to *The Best American Nonrequired Reading 2003*, the delightful Zadie Smith explains what Stegner meant. When you put pencil to paper, you "dramatize your belief in the miraculous, incommensurable existence of a society of six billion individuals. One of whom died three hundred and seventy-seven years ago while trying to freeze a chicken."

In this excerpt from a student essay, Reah Johnson addresses the topic "The Dumbing Down of America." Her "dramatization of belief" was written to be used as an original oratory in speech competition. Although she had already taken the ACT, Johnson's essay/oratory is an excellent example of how telling the truth about a common experience can make you more "likable." And, oddly enough, no chickens were killed (or frozen) in her dramatization.

Sunday, October 15. I am at the mall with a mission. No, not jeans, ice cream, CDs or cute boys. I am there to figure out the next four years of my academic life. Hundreds of booths are set up, each with eager college representatives passing out pamphlets, pinpointing information, and propagandizing anything pertaining to their school. It was the College Fair, but fair it wasn't. Some booths couldn't attract a single soul.

Being the clueless person that I am, I must have picked up a hundred pamphlets. It was at the end of my trek, though, when away from the mainstream I noticed *the* booth. Crowded with so many teens that I initially thought *Must be a party school.* I had to see for myself. Fighting through mobs of teenage girls and their mothers, I squinted to make out the university's name. "CLINIQUE

BONUS TIME." Not a renowned university, but a universally known cosmetics line.

Instead of learning about, say, the University of Michigan application process, the girls had chosen to learn about the application of "Sheer Sable" blush. It shouldn't come as a surprise, then, that media researcher Jean Kilbourne tells us the number one wish for girls ages eleven to seventeen is to be . . . on their high school speech team. You don't believe me, do you? Actually, what they really want has nothing to do with matters academic. They just want to be thinner. And, naturally, the number one wish for boys is to have a girlfriend who's well informed. . . . Did I say well informed? I meant to say well formed.

According to author Steve Allen, Americans are suffering from a mental incapacitation, and he's not talking only about teenage boys and girls. To be blunt, too many of us have become what H. L. Mencken refers to as the "Boobus Americanus," a bird too ignorant to know which way to fly. Well, it's time to wake up and fly right. Take a recent survey that revealed twelve-year-olds could name 5.2 alcoholic beverages but only 4.8 presidents. A third of high school students didn't know the United States had ever been involved in a war with Vietnam. Twenty-six percent of high school graduates couldn't identify Mexico on a map. And if you really want to be shocked, I could share with you my ACT scores. But then I would begin to cry and my new Clinique mascara would start to run.

Johnson's self-effacing humor (about her ACT score) and her playfulness with language increase her likability. But the true story of her visit to a College Fair is compelling—as an argument—because of the sources she quotes and the factual support she includes. And, let's face it, she is refreshingly honest.

Although it is unlikely that you will have much in the way of facts or quotes in your ACT essay, don't substitute goo for Google.

Avoid what is known as "sky is blue" evidence: for example, quoting the president of the United States saying, "Drug abuse is bad." Overstating the obvious is bad. When in doubt, stick with likable.

2. Stockpile the "Somethings" of Others

You may not have a relevant personal experience to share on a particular topic. What then? That's when you turn to the true story of someone else. You hear stories every day—from your parents, your teachers, your friends. The key is not only to stockpile those stories but also to remember the specific details that give the stories life.

In this student essay, Yasmin Mashhoon writes on the topic "The Media as a Freak Show." Her argument became that the media, too often, reflects who we are.

I was sitting in English class the other day and my teacher told us a story about his days as a student at the University of Nebraska. Somewhat bored one day, he said, he was lurking in the lunch line at Selleck Quadrangle. So, in order to entertain his friends and the girls behind them, he was doing his best—or should I say, his worst—impression of a mentally challenged person. He was successfully distorting his voice, face, and body when he looked up for a moment, and his eyes locked onto those of a member of the kitchen staff. My teacher described how he felt her eyes pierce right through him, and she said: "How would you feel if you really were that way?"

My teacher was immediately ashamed and he didn't say another word. Standing in that line all those years ago, he was ashamed that he was imitating someone different than he. At that moment, he made a personal decision to stop supporting the Freak Show.

Does the story ring true? Why? Perhaps because the details are not ones that would typically occur to a high school student. ACT readers are likely to react positively to this story both because of its uniqueness and because they want it to be true. You want an ACT reader to like you—to root for you.

The savvy student knows that the stories of others can be a valuable resource. After all, Gilda Radner's hyper pajama party characters were drawn, in part, from the work of Lily Tomlin's six-year-old alter ego Edith Ann. "And that's," as Edith Ann liked to say, "the truth."

Connect the Dots

"When you're acting, you ideally are out of control. In control of being out of control. And when you are directing, you should be in control. Somewhat out of control of being in control. But in control. And if you're trying to be out of control and somewhat in control of being out of control but out of control and, at the same time, in control but somewhat out of control of being in control but still in control, it makes you crazy."
—actor Warren Beatty, quoted in Bill Zehme's book *Intimate Strangers*

Beatty's convoluted logic notwithstanding, control matters. In writing persuasively, you need to have control of your arguments. You exercise this control by the choices you make. Those choices allow you to "connect the dots" in your essay. The process of "connecting the dots" means providing information, paying attention to it, and making sense of it. In short, you are giving form to arguments.

In discussing how to develop arguments, Aristotle said there are three ways to appeal to an audience: logical, emotional, and ethical proof. Of course, Aristotle was describing the art of public speaking. The principles, though, are just as important when you are trying to "connect the dots" as a writer. In other words, our persuasive power depends on our ability to reason, the emotions we are able to stir in the reader, and the reader's understanding of our character.

Logical Proof

You offer logical proof when you use sequence and analysis in your organizational pattern and factual evidence to prove your position. You are letting the reader in on how your thoughts connect. In the following passage, the student Ladan Jafari argues that the diet industry is taking control of too many lives.

Just pick up a magazine like *YM*, which, with no sense of irony, stands for young and modern. Throughout each issue the young and modern reader is subjected to the waiflike appearance of every model pictured. Kate Moss, for example, seems to be famous only for her skin and bones. And not surprisingly, in the last few pages of every issue there are series of advertisements about how to be a model, how to get "stronger, thicker, longer hair," and, of course, how to lose weight.

One weight-loss advertisement in particular caught my eye. For only twelve dollars you can own the Body Maker. The Body Maker promises: "Before you know it, you'll be going to the mall to get that cute bikini you always wished you could wear." Just ask Eve, a thirteen-year-old who writes to tell the Body Maker company: "Your product is awesome! I used to weigh 135 pounds. Now I weigh 115 pounds and still going down. Thank you for giving me my life back."

Guess what, Eve. You still need a life.

So how does Jafari "connect the dots"? Specific examples. Statistics. Satire. Are you persuaded by her approach? Is the proof logical to you? What about an ACT essay reader staring at a computer screen, eyes glazed over, nibbling on Krispy Kremes? In the immortal words of comic and author Spike Milligan: "Gobble gobble glup glup munch munch munch."

"You've got to _want_ to connect the dots, Mr. Michaelson."

Emotional Proof

You offer emotional proof when you "strike a chord" in your reader by appealing to a sense of patriotism, family, justice, or the like. Risks come with emotional appeals. The reader might think you are silly or superficial. The traditional advice to young writers has never been more true: show, don't tell. Study this example from Molly Dunn, a student writing on the topic "Now is the time to rehumanize America."

> When I was a fifth grader at S. Y. Jackson Elementary School, my best friend Sarah was the typical nerd. One day, when the teacher was out of the room for a while, the class bully decided it would be fun to lock Sarah out of the classroom. As her best friend, I could not stand by and

let this happen. I stood outside, locked out of the classroom with her. Sarah was so hurt by the bully's actions that she was bawling. Then, one by one, my entire class came outside to stand with us. This experience was a lesson that I never would have received had I been attending school through my home computer. Sitting at a computer all day, a child might learn to read, write, and recite multiplication tables, but she will be estranged from the world of other children.

Do you think that Dunn's story would "strike a chord" with most readers? What percentage of English teachers (the readers of the ACT essay) do you think were bullied at some time during their childhood? On the other hand, what if Dunn had written the following:

Bullies often hurt people's feelings. They shouldn't be allowed to pick on people. If we allow this brutish behavior to continue, it will make us less human.

Ethical Proof

Lack of specificity weakens writing. Concrete details empower. Dunn's story about Sarah and the bully serves as ethical proof for the student writer as well. You offer ethical (or personal) proof when you show the reader that you have a natural honesty about you. The reader must sense a strong value system and an unwillingness to compromise when it comes to doing the right thing.

In the following excerpt from a student essay, Amaris Singer explains the need to "connect the dots" in our thinking. The ethical proof comes both from her extensive knowledge of the subject matter and from the clear sense that, to her, doing what is right matters.

Recently, I visited the Chicago Art Institute, and I came upon one of my favorite paintings, George Seurat's *Sunday Afternoon on the Island of La Grande Jatte*. As a nineteenth-century French neo-impressionist, Seurat's development of pointillism changed the way we view the world. If you stand a few inches away from the painting, you can see dots of pure color juxtaposed on a white canvas. But if you move away from the painting, you learn Seurat's true intention. His primary concern was linear perspective, how the dots connected and their relationship to the accumulated shadows that surrounded them. We need to see those connections. Our government agencies should connect the dots that surround them. Investors and businesses should be wary of dots that look too good to be true. And each of us, as individuals, must step back and see the big picture.

After you have completed any piece of writing, you, too, need to step back and see the big picture. Do your arguments make sense? Did you "connect the dots"?

> *"If a cat has kittens in an oven, does that make them biscuits?"*
> —Malcolm X

Get Your Backup

The author Richard Saul Wurman points out that "a weekday edition of the *New York Times* contains more information than the average person was likely to come across in a lifetime in seventeenth-century England."

How much information will the reader come across in your ACT essay? More than a Cro-Magnon man during his brief cave stay? Actually, your goal should not be related to how much information but to how good that information is. In some ways, the "Get Your Backup" strategy reinforces the principles outlined in the "Connect the Dots" strategy. The information that you provide to back up your position has to make sense.

Some have suggested that you write and memorize a couple of "general" essays in advance of the exam. You can then have those essays evaluated beforehand for content and correctness. The strategy is to pick universal topics like justice or freedom or responsibility. You simply apply what you have written to the specific requirements of the ACT essay topic. Warning: this strategy can backfire badly if your essay sounds too "canned" or if the links you make to the topic assigned are tenuous.

Remember that the readers don't expect a know-it-all approach. What they do want is one or two excellent examples. Make sure those examples are specific and memorable.

1. Be Specific

"All my life I wanted to be somebody. Now I see I should have been more specific."
—Lily Tomlin

Consider the advice of Jane Mallison, who has graded standardized essays since 1979—more essays than she can remember. She said, "Use specifics. So many mediocre essays are written decently in terms of sentence structure, but they say it blandly, or they don't give supporting details."

One student wrote about how America is becoming a "nation of spectators." She recalls a visit to Ellis Island. Pay special attention to her use of specific details.

I thought about what it meant to be a spectator when I traveled to New York last summer. I visited Ellis Island because my great-grandfather was one of the twelve million immigrants who passed through there. Embedded in the steel of the memorial, I found his name. And I remembered again his journey. To escape persecution, my great-grandfather left his family, friends, and belongings in Poland. He fled by riding through the night on a bicycle to avoid detection, and by hiding in the swamps outside of Krakow.

My great-grandfather loved being an American. But his life in his newly adopted home was not an easy one. He sold fruit, painted houses, and worked in a naval shipyard. He did whatever life demanded to make sure that his descendants would someday enjoy freedom. My great-grandfather would not have allowed me to become a spectator.

2. Be Memorable

As discussed earlier, the essay instructions will most likely ask you for an example to support your position. You should be collecting memorable examples that have numerous applications. A memorable example usually contains humor, action, controversy, or an unexpected twist.

Do you remember hearing about the twenty-seven-year-old adventurer in Colorado who became hopelessly pinned by a boulder? The boulder, weighing an estimated 800 pounds, trapped his right arm against the cliff face. The man, Aron Ralston, made a choice: to take his dull pocketknife and to cut off his arm—a choice to save his life. After describing the harrowing details in a gripping press conference in Grand Junction, Colorado, Ralston returned to his hospital room. *Sports Illustrated* writer Rick Reilly was there. According to Reilly, all that Ralston said was, "I wish I could have been funnier."

Is this story memorable? Do you think you might be asked to respond to a question that touches on a topic involving difficult choices? Does the attitude of the person making that difficult choice matter?

True, the ACT essay could be funnier. But, hey, you don't need a dull pocketknife to survive. A sharp number two pencil will do nicely.

Serve Your Sentence

*"Like a superhighway, the sentence is a triumph
of engineering: the stately capital letter, the procession
of words in their proper order, every arch and tunnel,
bridge and buttress is fitted to its job."*
—Patricia T. O'Connor, *Words Fail Me*

Because you have little time for "triumphant" construction, you don't want to find yourself on a road to nowhere. Struggling to merge thought and topic. Searching for the next period. Lost.

The ACT readers consider sentence variety as one factor in evaluating your essay. Therefore, so should you. Use your ear to tell if you need emergency sentence repair. In his book *Write to Learn*, Donald M. Murray discusses the importance of writing with your ear. As a newspaper consultant, he explains to editors how he can pick out the best writers in the city room. Murray simply looks to see "which writers' lips were moving as they wrote." Of the two paragraphs that follow, which is more pleasing to your ear?

The ancient African Lesu tribe made boys dodge burning branches. The branches were hurled at them by their fathers. Then the boys were men. The Tlingit culture made girls live for an entire year in a dark room. The girls had to pluck and sew duck feathers. Boys in New Zealand had to kill sharks. The boys would venture into the ocean with just a knife. The Ubatu slaughtered wild boars. They used wooden spikes.

To become a man in the ancient African Lesu tribe, a boy had to dodge burning branches hurled at him by his father. To become a woman in the Tlingit culture, a girl had to live for an entire year in a dark room plucking and sewing duck feathers. In New Zealand, a youth had to take a knife, venture into the ocean, and kill a shark. And for the Ubatu, the challenge was slaughtering a wild boar, using a wooden spike.

(Please note: Today, such rites of passage may seem ill-advised. Yet every year two million of America's youth engage in their own barbaric rite. Herded into crowded assembly rooms, huddled behind tiny desks, armed with only two soft-lead pencils, these adolescents embark on a perilous mission: to choose the best of thousands of possible ovals as they undergo hours of rigorous torture. That's right, they take the ACT!)

As you read the excerpts, you should have become aware of the importance of sentence variety. Clearly, the second paragraph flows more smoothly. The choppy sentences of the first paragraph make the reader seasick. That's why writers use clauses and verbals. That's why they combine sentences. They break patterns that might become boring and predictable. That does not mean you should crank out only long, complex sentences. Carefully crafted sentences are difficult to construct given the time constraints of the ACT. A well-written paragraph will have both long and short sentences.

Long before the creation of *Grammar Rock*, Ernest Hemingway took up residence at Conjunction Junction (that is, when he wasn't mass-producing simple, pared-down sentences). Hemingway imitators have parodied the sameness of his compound sentences.

And you can stop your story the way you stop a life and you do not do it and afterwards you are not sorry and all of which and none of which has anything to do with glory and honor and courage and booting empty beer cans in

*Ketchum, Idaho, and the judgment comes and the
compound sentence is served and sixty-two years become a
life and then one day you run out of . . . "ands."*

Even if you didn't know the term "compound sentence," you would
realize that the repetitiveness of the Hemingway parody is too
much. Learning the terms, however, should not be your strategy
now. As David Byrne, formerly of the Talking Heads, said, "Facts
are useless in emergencies." OK, Byrne wasn't talking about the
ACT. But it is an emergency.

Take comfort. Chances are that the first thought, the first sentence that occurs to you will be your best. Writing teacher Peter
Elbow calls this the power of "raw first-draft writing." Elbow
believes that if you are excited and involved in the meaning of what
you are saying, you need not worry. For the most part, Elbow is
right. Worry is your enemy.

Your worst enemy, though, is the belief that you need to sound
a certain way. That's when your voice, your truth, turns into "in
sum, therefore, it can be noted that . . ." You shouldn't sound like a
prisoner of pedantry. You should sound like you.

Remember: the ear doesn't lie. Nor does the mouth hear much.
And the nose? Forget about it. But we digress. If you want to know
if your writing flows nicely, your best bet is always to read aloud
anything that you write.

*"No style is good that is not fit to be spoken or read aloud
with effect."*
—William Hazlitt

Camouflage
Airy Persiflage

Cartoon legends Rocky and Bullwinkle befuddled a generation of young viewers with obscure literary allusions. Their self-effacing use of the phrase "airy persiflage" in an episode, for example, paid homage to another famous duo: Gilbert and Sullivan. In Gilbert and Sullivan's *The Mikado*, the character Ko-Ko asks, "Is this a time for airy persiflage?"

Ko-Ko's question is an important one for you to answer. Airy persiflage, of course, is nothing more than light banter. Empty chatter. You would like your essay to be something more. Something more than *bandying about boisterous badinage*. You should, therefore, incorporate literary allusions. Try to avoid relying, though, on lines lifted from light operas. The rarely used allusion should be just that.

The key to this strategy, then, is to choose a recognizable literary passage that will apply to a number of different essay questions.

Consider a line from Shakespeare's *Hamlet*: "There is nothing either good or bad, but thinking makes it so."

Here Hamlet draws the distinction between perception and reality. Hamlet knows that what is thought matters more than what is. In developing a strategy to employ this quote, it might help you to think about the three kinds of truth: your truth, the reader's truth, and *the* truth. In discussing almost any topic, after all, you can address the gap that exists between the perceived truth and the reality.

Study the following approach that includes Hamlet's line.

A major benefit of Prozac is the so-called placebo effect. Even if the drug has no actual physiological effect, the *New York Times* reports a high number of people who pull out of depression anyway. Some cases of depression, especially those caused by a lack of confidence, can cure themselves if the people believe they should be cured.

Doctor Hamlet would agree: "There is nothing either good or bad, but thinking makes it so." The *Times* notes cases of people who were really taking sugar pills and were cured, literally, by the name of the drug. Their "thinking" made it so.

Clearly, Hamlet's observation can be applied to many topics.

General Hamlet, for example, might argue that it is difficult to win a war without the people's perception that the conflict is justified.

Professor Hamlet might argue that people must "think" that teacher pay raises are warranted for those raises to happen.

Sports Illustrated writer Rick Reilly accurately explains the difference between perception and reality:

> *YOUR SLUGGER is a steroid-dripping cheat. MY SLUGGER has made a major off-season commitment to reshaping his body.*

> *YOUR TEAM'S FANS are the kind of single-toothed vermin that real vermin cross the street to avoid. MY TEAM'S FANS are fiercely loyal.*

Sportswriter Hamlet would agree, don't you think?

. . . .

Four Tips

1. Select Not-So-Familiar Quotes from Familiar Sources

You may not want to rehash John F. Kennedy's famous "Ask not what your country can do for you . . ." call to a generation. That call has been trumpeted far too many times for freshness. On the other hand, if you are writing on an education topic, it might be helpful to remember Kennedy's less-known but chilling observation: "A child miseducated is a child lost."

2. Make Creative Connections

When you incorporate a literary allusion, you are connecting yourself to the reader. You now have something in common. If you can playfully strengthen that relationship, all the better.

Oscar Wilde argued that there is a lot more to stupidity than most people imagine. Reality television is going about the business of proving Wilde wrong.

This example has the delicious ambiguity of the Wilde witticism, plus it plays into the likely bias that the reader will have against reality television. And even an ardent fan of "Survivor" knows it's a guilty pleasure at best.

Now compare the following two sentences:

Critics were unkind in reviewing the plays of Tennessee Williams in his later years.

A crass menagerie of critics urged Tennessee Williams to take one last ride on a streetcar named retire.

The first sentence is merely correct. The second sentence makes a creative connection between his plays—*Glass Menagerie* and *A Streetcar Named Desire*—and the criticism of Williams by reviewers. Which sentence would be more memorable to a reader on a hot tin roof?

3. Tack-On Quotes Are Tacky

Avoid responding to topics with generic-sounding quotes. Contrived choices seldom survive scrutiny.

Winston Churchill once said: "Never give up. Never give up. Never give up." Similarly, I didn't give up when I was cut from the soccer team.

Ah yes, from Mia Hamm to mea culpa. Be careful of the word *similarly* as a transitional link. Chances are slim that the two situations compared are at all alike. Take you and Winston Churchill. Please.

Another example:

My friends often find it difficult to escape peer pressure. "To thine own self be true" must have been easier in Shakespeare's day when it was possible to "know thyself."

Avoid piggybacking overused quotes. Especially when one isn't attributed to the right source. According to *Bartlett's Familiar Quotations*, the advice "Know thyself" is taken from an inscription at the Delphic Oracle. Know thy quotes.

Martin Luther King had a dream. So do I.

Enough said?

4. Be Simple; Be Direct; Affirm

Never say, "In the words of so-and-so," or, "These thoughts were never better expressed than by so-and-so." Say instead, "So-and-so was right."

Beat writer Jack Kerouac was right: "Walking on water wasn't built in a day."

Sample Allusions Not Widely Known but with Universal Appeal

If you memorize ten quotes that apply to a great number of topics, you increase your chances for a memorable essay. Consider the following examples.

When you need to write about a personal hero or someone else you admire:

"She had never been especially impressed by the heroics of the people convinced that they are about to change the world. She

was more awed by the heroism of those who are willing to struggle to make one small difference after another."
—Pulitzer Prize–winning columnist Ellen Goodman, referring to herself

For a topic that requires discussing the morality of a decision:

"Aim above morality. Be not simply good, be good for something."
—philosopher Henry David Thoreau

For any topic that touches on hypocrisy:

"You can no more become a Christian by going to church than you can become an automobile by sleeping in the garage."
—humorist Garrison Keillor

Now go find your own quotes. Search through your favorite books or pick up a book that collects quotes. Other sources to turn to are the many books that anthologize columns by syndicated writers (Ellen Goodman, Anna Quindlen, Dave Barry, and so forth).

Remember: in the military, soldiers wear camouflage to blend in with their surroundings. Literary allusions should dress up an essay without drawing attention to themselves. Does Dante need a brightly colored do-rag? Probably not.

In *The Mikado*, Ko-Ko's question was ignored, remaining unanswered until now.

Eenie-meenie, chili-beanie, the spirits are about to speak.

Yes and no.

Avoid Slang-uishing

By the time you read this book, the schizzle will have lost its sizzle. Language evolves, even if you don't. What was once a simple kiss became "sucking face" became "tonsil hockey" became "tongue sushi"—a sort of cold rice kiss described by language guru William Safire as "a mutual rolling-up of teenage linguae engaged in lubricious osculation." Who says that romance is dead?

Someday, your inability to communicate with your children will frustrate you, the way your parents suffer now. After all, you're too young to remember a time when teenagers thought everything was "copacetic." And the beat goes on.

In fact, the average ACT reader doesn't know a nizzle from a nozzle. Is it any wonder that a high court judge in London recently ruled that rap should be treated as "a foreign language"?

Keep this ruling in mind as you write your essay. The ACT company trains readers to consider word choice as one criterion in essay evaluation. They can't fairly evaluate what they don't understand. But being understood is not enough. You want to be appreciated, by golly.

Word Choice Matters

Here are four suggestions:

1. Just Say No to Sesquipedalian

You may be tempted to dabble in fancy words. Foreign words. Restrain yourself. The *New Yorker* illustrates how confusing tickling your fancy can be.

The denouement of the impromptu powwow convened at the accouchement of Sister Jane was that, Deo volente, the nuns would be separated by a thick purdah from that handsome young horseman Dick at the next gymkhana . . .

And we all know how painful a "thick purdah" can be. Or, at the very least, uncomfortable. Preferring long words does not make you a better writer—just less clear. Of the 701 words in Lincoln's Second Inaugural Address, 505 are words of one syllable and 122 are words of two syllables. Honest . . .

2. Yo, Can U Pliz Write English

Don't let the undue familiarity of online lingo creep into your formal writing. True, insider phrases and abbreviated words do fit into the electronic format. But the ACT essay requires appropriateness. Linguistic shortcuts, shoddy grammar, and absent punctuation may work with "sk8r boi" but not with rdr grrl. Or rdr boi.

In *USA Today*, Steve Friess told the story of a father who kept his children from chatting with friends online. Why? The father spotted a problem in his fifteen-year-old son's summer job application: "I want 2 b a counselor because i love 2 work with kids."

And would you like fries with that?

3. Practice Verb-Reliance

In his journals, transcendentalist Ralph Waldo Emerson mused on what it meant to be a good writer:

All writing should be selection in order to drop every dead word. . . . Then all words will be sprightly, and every sentence a surprise.

Emerson cherished spirited writing—the unexpected moments of delight that make us want to read on. But how do you create these moments in your essay?

Former baseball great Reggie Jackson once said of pitcher Tom Seaver: "Blind people come to the game just to listen to his fastball."

What if Jackson had said, instead, that Seaver had a really good fastball? Would anyone remember Jackson's words? You don't want your writing to be forgettable. So . . . *make high-energy verbs your fastball.* High-energy verbs push paragraphs forward. They add vitality and momentum (more sprightly than passive voice, Emerson would say). They shorten sentences.

She aced the math exam. (active voice)

The math exam was aced by her. (passive voice)

Don't assume, however, that passive voice is always wrong. Passive voice can create a more conversational tone—up to a point. In *The Comic Toolbox*, John Vorhaus demonstrates what happens when passive voice goes awry. Enjoy his description of a love triangle's tragic end.

Suddenly, the door was opened by the husband. . . . A gun was held by him. Some screams were screamed and angry words exchanged. Jealousy was felt by the man by whom the gun was held. Firing of the gun was done by him. The flying of bullets took place. Impact was felt by bodies. The floor was hit by bodies. Remorse was then felt by the man by whom the gun was held. The gun was turned upon himself.

The rest, as Vorhaus might say, was shown on "CSI."

Tip: don't overuse forms of the verb "to be": *is, am, are, was, were, be, been.*

Make strong verb choices. They should be striking. Unleash fastballs. Study the following passage from S. J. Perelman. In his short story "Farewell, My Lovely Appetizer," Perelman uses action verbs to move his detective around the city.

*I hired a hack to Wanamaker's, cut over to Third, walked up
toward Fourteenth. At Twelfth, a mink-faced jasper made up
as a street cleaner tailed me for a block, drifted into a dairy
restaurant. At Thirteenth somebody dropped a sour tomato
out of a third-story window, missing me by inches. I doubled
back to Wanamaker's, hopped a bus up Fifth to Madison
Square, and switched to a cab down Fourth, where the
secondhand bookshops elbow each other like dirty urchins.*

4. Find the Chiefest Words

As poet Emily Dickinson advised, you must choose "the chiefest
word, the best word." Choosing the "chiefest word" stimulates the
reader's appetite. In his book *The Elements of Expression*, Arthur
Plotnik discusses the stimulating words found in the menus of
trendy restaurants. Indeed, Plotnik provides food for thought.
Restaurateurs often find imaginative ways to take your American
Express card to its gastronomic limits. Otherwise, why would you
order "roasted ratatouille terrine with roasted garlic, garlic flowers
and virgin olive oil, Napoleon of dehydrated curly cabbage with
autumn forest mushrooms"? . . . yum-yum.

Furthermore, finding the "chiefest word" first can shape an essay
for you. Consider the following situation.

You and a friend linger in the candy aisle of your neighborhood
grocery store. Your friend furtively stuffs Snickers into his cargo
pants. You realize that the manager of the store has been watching
the theft and now heads toward you. As the manager grabs your
arm, your friend escapes through the front door. The manager gives
you a choice: you can either tell him the name of your friend or he
will turn you over to the police as a shoplifter. You think it over.
Betrayal or punishment?

Later, you want to write a story about this difficult decision, but
you wonder if there is a word to describe exactly what happened.
The word you are searching for is *dilemma*, a situation involving
two choices—both of them bad.

Such a word can be at the heart of successful writing. Take the Siberian dilemma, for example. In his novel *Gorky Park*, Martin Cruz Smith tells the story of a young gymnastics teacher in Siberia. While fishing on a lake, the teacher falls through the ice. The temperature is minus forty degrees. His dilemma: if he stays in the water he will freeze to death in thirty or forty seconds, and if he crawls out he will freeze to death immediately. He will be ice.

Smith writes: "He looked up at us; I'll never forget that look. He couldn't have been in the water for more than five seconds when he pulled himself out. But he got out, that was the important thing. He didn't just wait to die."

You, too, encounter many difficult choices in life. You are not, however, facing death in Siberia. You are facing the ACT essay. You can let things happen to you or you can make them happen. Learning to write well is the choice that makes words happen. Learning to write well is the choice to pull yourself out. It is the decision to take control of your future.

Now isn't that just jim-dandy?

Try Profiling

> *"Pure writing is the most rewarding of all because it is constantly accompanied by a voice that repeats, 'Why am I writing this?' Then, and only then, can the writer hope for his finest achievement: the voice of the reader uttering its complement, 'Why am I reading this?'"*
> —Steve Martin, *Fierce Pajamas*

If you read detective novels or watch television crime shows, you are familiar with the role of a profiler. The profiler analyzes data to forecast the day, time, and place a crime is likely to occur in order to prevent it from happening. You should be a profiler too. You already know the crime you are attempting to analyze. Unfortunately, the ACT can't be prevented, but there is data for you to consider. So, what do you know? You know why an ACT grader reads your writing: to assign your essay a score from 1 to 6. (The reader's grading system, or rubric, is discussed in the Practice Essays section.)

Do you really believe, though, that the readers are completely objective? With apologies to Pink Floyd, all in all, it's just another rubric in the wall. Every experience the graders have had—or haven't had—colors their evaluation of your essay. Suppose you write an essay on the topic of "love." If you asked the readers to define love, you would have as many different definitions as you had readers. Some would say love is affection, some, an affliction. And the images that you choose for your essay create in each reader an association with some real-life experience. For example, the image of a bicycle may remind you of your first solo trip to the grocery store. The reader may think, instead, of Lance Armstrong's battle with cancer.

And now that graders are sitting in front of their home computers, you may have to compete with some unexpected distractions: screaming children, reruns of "Matlock," a migraine headache. And, unfortunately, a reader is affected by the quality of the essay read before yours. Would you rather follow the efforts of the next Updike or the next up-the-creek? Chance and circumstance happen to us all.

So what do you do? As always, write the truth. Remember, at the same time, the strongest connection between writer and reader is simple humanity. The key, then, is to find the common ground. You may spend your every waking moment thinking about skateboarding. Believe it or not, the hired graders have other interests. On the other hand, rambling on about how you want to solve the world's problems makes you seem obsequious. You're against drug abuse. Now there's a shocker.

Keep in mind the advice from E. B. White discussed earlier in this book. Don't write about man. Write about *a* man. Rhetoricians have long known people are more persuaded by examples than by any other form of proof. They know you can lie with statistics. And testimonials are always suspect. But if something bad happened to Joe down the block, then "dangit, something must be done." Apply this rhetorical wisdom to your essay. Write about a person. Simple humanity. Study the following two quotations:

> "To be a child is to live in the fleeting joy of existence."
> —former U.N. Secretary General Dag Hammarskjold

> "What is childhood but a series of humiliating injustices that you spend the rest of your life avenging?"
> —comedian Colin Quinn

Readers should be able to relate to you. Which of the preceding two quotations would you say better set the tone for your telling of a childhood incident? The correct answer is both (except for the vengeance part). You may write about a childhood spent on the outskirts of hope but always hopeful for tomorrow. Most ACT readers have experienced humiliating injustices. They would like to believe in possibility.

A final thought: grading is drudgery. The readers lose the desire to go on. Distress sets in. Countless essays come and go on the computer screen. And yet, the readers must continue.

Two Suggestions to Make Everyone's Life More Pleasant

1. Primacy: The First Cut Is the Deepest

You know the commercial that says, "You never get a second chance to make a first impression." From the first sentence, you want the reader to be thinking that your essay could score a 6. A secondary purpose of the first sentence is to get the grader to read the next sentence. If your first sentence isn't a "grabber," the grader may skim the rest of your essay. Consider the opening sentences from the essays that follow. Do they make you want to read the second sentence?

> "*Many delights have accrued from the recent plebiscite here, not the least of which is that we have elected our normal quota of dead people, Lyndon LaRouche followers, freelance fruitloops, and folks whose names sound like someone famous.*"
> —Molly Ivins, "Political Asylum"

"My daddy down in Georgia told me, 'Son, take pride in your work, don't honk at old people, and never read a Civil War novel longer than Red Badge of Courage.'"
—Roy Blount Jr., "Shoe-Shoeing Lit"

"SAT scores are plummeting, college graduates can't read, and Americans are paying good money for bell-bottoms again."
—Bill Maher, "Are People Getting Stupider?"

2. Recency: We Were Kidding; the Last Cut Is the Deepest

Research reveals that we better remember what we read first and last in an essay than we recall everything in between. As it turns out, though, the last sentence stays with us longer than the first. The importance, then, of the last sentence in your essay can't be overstated. You should allocate your exam time so that your essay doesn't end in an unfinished sentence or an ugly smudge. The last sentence should round out and dismiss the thought. But it also should conclude your essay with a bang, not a whimper. You want the grader to leap from the chair and shout, "Huzzah! Huzzah! That essay was a real humdinger!" Or some such nonsense.

Read the following "last" sentences from professional essay writers:

"Seize it and let it seize you up aloft even, till your eyes burn out and drop; let your musky flesh fall off in shreds, and let your very bones unhinge and scatter, loosened over fields, over fields and woods, lightly, thoughtless, from any height at all, from as high as eagles."
—Annie Dillard, "Living Like Weasels"

"A man and his body are like a boy and the buddy who has a driver's license and the use of his father's car for the evening; he goes along, gratefully, for the ride."
—John Updike, *The Disposable Rocket*

"Apart from what any critic had to say about my writing, I knew I had succeeded where it counted when my mother finished reading my book and gave me her verdict: 'So easy to read.'"
—Amy Tan, "Mother Tongue"

Earlier in her "Mother Tongue" essay, Tan explains that she envisions her mother as the reader. Tan wanted to capture "what language ability tests can never reveal: her intent, her passion, her imagery, the rhythms of her speech and the nature of her thoughts."

Tan's mother will not be grading your essay. Envision an English teacher who wants to like you, to like your essay. Give the reader a humdinger.

F. Scott Fitzgerald was right: "You can stroke people with words."

Prethink, Methinks

"He was deeply in love when she spoke—he thought he heard bells, as if she were a garbage truck backing up. Her vocabulary was as bad as, like, whatever—but she had a deep, throaty, genuine laugh, like that sound a dog makes just before he throws up. He fell for her like his heart was a mob informant and she was the East River; she grew on him like E. coli and he was room temperature Canadian beef."

—Phil Proctor, *Funny Times*

As you may have guessed, Proctor is making sport of high school writers. He composed his own essay with analogies and metaphors taken from the actual writing of students like you. Or should we say, like underpants in a dryer without Cling Free. So before you start writing amok, "proctor" yourself. But how?

Prethink Your Essay

The time constraints for the ACT essay make painstaking revision impossible. Even limited rethinking of what you have written will be difficult. Therefore, prethinking is probably your most effective strategy.

Before you put pencil to paper, take a few minutes to think about the assigned topic. Choose a central idea that you will formulate into a thesis statement. Then decide on related evidence and supporting examples. Now ask yourself: will the English teacher sitting in judgment of my ideas find them compelling?

If the answer to that question is yes, begin to articulate those ideas in outline form. Make sure that you have a clear thesis statement and that all of the ideas are connected to it. Don't write anything down until you have spoken the words aloud under your breath. Let your ear be the final editor.

Tip: practice prethinking essays several times before the actual exam. The most important practice session is the night before. Writing a complete essay under game conditions the night before programs your brain. In other words, sit in silence at a desk with a number two pencil. No music blaring in the background. No cellphone chats. No testus interruptus.

As you practice prethinking essays, ask yourself four questions:

1. **Am I clear?** The goal is not to hide your meaning in cleverness. The reader will spend only a few minutes on your essay. Vague thoughts or misleading information confuse the reader. Do you want a grumpy reader mumbling, "What the . . . ?"

2. **Am I precise?** Don't drown in the stream of consciousness. Are you saying exactly what you mean? The key is not how many details but how well chosen. Suppose that you're writing about your friend who loves words. What is missing from the following passage?

   My friend is into crossword puzzles. Learning all those weird words makes him happy. I've never heard of some of them. Only one other kid in the school does crosswords. This very strange girl.

   Now read the passage from P. G. Wodehouse. Wodehouse names the people and provides examples of words familiar to crossword aficionados. Even if the reader knows nothing of these puzzles, the precise details employed by Wodehouse draw the reader in.

George spent a not unhappy life . . . doing crossword puzzles. By the time he was thirty he knew more about Eli, the prophet, Ra, the Sun God, and the bird Emu than anybody else in the country except Susan Blake, the vicar's daughter, who had also taken up the solving of crossword puzzles and was the first girl in Worcestershire to find out the meaning of stearine *and* crepuscular.

By the way, *crepuscular* refers to twilight, hence, imperfectly clear. Hmm . . .

3. **Am I interesting?** Share your humanity. Write about people as if you're composing music. No dissonance. Never off-key. The sentences should please the ear. And the stories should engage the reader.

Study the excerpt from Lorrie Moore's short story "How to Become a Writer." Although the passage is fiction, learn from her storytelling ability. Give life to your true stories with the same playfulness.

Tell your roommate your great idea, your great exercise of imaginative power: a transformation of Melville to contemporary life. It will be about monomania and the fish-eat-fish world of life insurance in Rochester, New York. The first line will be "Call me Fishmeal," and it will feature a menopausal suburban husband named Richard, who because he is so depressed all the time is called "Mopey Dick" by his witty wife, Elaine.

Do you find the narrator in the story interesting? Do you want to read more about her? Of course. The writing is fresh. It flows. And the narrator is engaging. These are desirable qualities in any piece of writing.

4. Am I genuine?

> *"Well, apparently that's what was missing from my other pieces, my opinions."*
> —Rory Gilmore, "Gilmore Girls"

When the character Rory reviews a ballet performance on an episode of "Gilmore Girls," she eviscerates the lead ballerina. Rory describes her as a hippo, and there is talk of kicking and wincing. The *Yale Daily News* then prints the review much to the dismay of the ballerina. The lesson for Rory, budding young journalist: your version of the truth can upset people.

Clearly, you don't want to upset the ACT readers. Arguing unpopular positions may impress your college professors one day, but rein yourself in for the ACT. You can't safely predict the politics of your readers. Their biases. Their open-mindedness. For example, you might not want to say, "You know, the Unabomber made a few good points."

We hope you are a good person (you were good enough to buy this book, weren't you?). Let your innate decency be at the heart of what you write. Elie Wiesel tells the story of a rabbi who said that when we cease to live and go before our Creator, the question asked of us will not be why we did not become a messiah, a famous leader, or answer the great mysteries of life. The question will simply be: "Why did you not become you?" When the time comes and you finally have to put pencil to paper, write your truth. Become you.

Take the Shot

t's 1998. The Cleveland Cavaliers battle the Chicago Bulls. Seventh and deciding game in the Eastern Conference championship. Three seconds to play. Cleveland leads 100 to 99. Michael Jordan takes the ball and dribbles toward the key. He pulls up from inside the circle. Craig Ehlo, one of Cleveland's top defenders, leaps out to block him, but Jordan seems to hang there in midair until Ehlo falls away. Then Jordan releases the sweetest jumper you ever saw. A video highlight for the ages. Forever known as "the Shot."

Bulls 101, Cavaliers 100.

And what did Michael Jordan say he thought about when he got the ball?

Nothing.

He just did it the same way he did it countless other times in his life.

No thinking.

Take heart. You may not be the Michael Jordan of essayists, but you have written before. Many times. We're not, however, recommending "no thinking." As suggested earlier, you would be wise to

"prethink" your essay. Just don't get caught in an all-too-common trap: if a little thinking is good, a lot must be better. Especially when those extra thoughts are not about the task at hand. Negative ones, for example: "I should have prepared," "I never do well on essay tests," "Even doctors have more legible handwriting," "I'm a bigger loser than Bobby Brady in that ice-cream-eating contest."

Don't give in to your misgivings. Based on twenty years of research on overthinking, University of Michigan professor Susan Nolen-Hoeksen suggests that at the first sign of a problem, you should pull away temporarily and then you should strategize. Because you have limited minutes to complete the essay, don't pull away for too long. You need to refocus immediately on the question asked. No mooncalfing. No lollydolling. Attack that topic with—to borrow a phrase from reviewer Robert Bianco—the fervor of a Soviet tractor documentary.

Dissecting each word in that question, though, can create a different kind of overthinking: the paralysis of analysis, some have called it. Laboring over each word in writing your answer can be equally troublesome. Endless ruminating is seldom illuminating—a lesson learned by Nicolas Cage as the character Charlie Kaufman in the film *Adaptation*. Charlie (in voice-over) ruminates:

> *To begin. To begin. How to start. I'm hungry. I should get coffee. Coffee would help me think. I should write something first, then reward myself with coffee. Coffee and a muffin. OK. So I need to establish the themes. Maybe banana-nut. That's a good muffin.*

Forget muffins. Learn, instead, from the experiences of writers gone by. When asked what he considered to be a day's work, Oscar Wilde replied, "This morning I inserted a comma; this afternoon I shall take it out again."

Now is not the time to lapse into a comma. Take the shot.

PRACTICE ESSAYS WITH ANNOTATIONS

*"You're not the boss of me now. You're not the boss of me . . .
and you're not so big."*
—"Malcolm in the Middle" theme song, by
They Might Be Giants

OK, you're not so big. In fact, you still feel like a mediocre Malcolm in the middle of a muddle. You don't produce well under pressure. Or you have a lot of personal problems. Or you come from a family where cousins marry.

Well, you know the old saying: if you fall off a horse, fire the stable manager (or something like that). In preparing for the ACT essay, think of yourself as the "unstable" manager of your future. Stop horsing around. You're already good at that.

The stakes have been raised. These practice essay questions should help. They will help more if you answer the questions *before* you read the example essays!

Work with one sample essay at a time. Compare what you have written with both of the examples for each topic. The sample essays are not perfect. They were written by students just like you. Their purpose is to provoke thought. You need to define your weaknesses in order to improve in those areas. You need to shore up your strengths. You need to focus. Otherwise, you will share the fate of author Stephen Leacock's famous horseman in the short story "Gertrude the Governess," who "rode off madly in all directions."

After all, the ACT, whether we like it or not, is "so big."

Preparing for the Practice Essays

The ACT writing test is a thirty-minute, paper-and-pencil essay designed to evaluate your writing skills—specifically those you've already studied in high school English classes and those you will cover in freshman college composition courses. Although thirty minutes may not seem like much (or may seem like a lot), at least it's five minutes longer than the SAT's twenty-five-minute essay. Because you won't have time to draft, revise, and recopy your essay, you'll want to spend some minutes organizing your thoughts and planning your essay before you start writing. You should also save a few minutes at the end to quickly review what you've written and make any last-minute changes.

The test itself consists of a writing prompt that will give you two sides of an issue. For example, some researchers say that the high school day begins too early, that teenagers don't function well at 8 A.M. (no surprise there, right?). On the other hand, some say that we should start the school day early to leave time for sports and other activities in the afternoon. The writing prompt will ask you to support one or the other of these two views, or come up with a new position of your own. Which side you support is not important; how you support your position is.

In the following section you will find a sampling of student essays. They were written in response to some typical ACT prompts. No one can guess in advance what a prompt will be about, but the ACT does promise that the topics will be relevant to high school students (in other words, you won't have to write about Social Security). Pay close attention to these essays to find out where the students went right (and wrong).

The Readers Use a Rubric; You Should Too

The readers of your essay are trained to look for clear and consistent competence. The list that follows should be your guide as you practice.

- Address the specific writing task.
- Have a well-organized response.
- Include appropriate and fully developed supporting ideas.
- Have sentence variety.
- Include specific details.
- Employ strong verb choices.

Understanding the Annotated Essays

Each sample essay in this section has four parts.

1. Topic

No study aid will have the exact topic you must address on the ACT. All of the topics selected for inclusion here are similar to the modus operandi of the ACT.

2. Essay

Students just like you wrote the sample essays. You will be surprised by the shortcomings in some of the essays, inspired by the strengths of others. Learn from each of them. Apply what you learn.

3. Critique

An independent evaluator scores each essay. The feedback is meant to be representative of what a typical English teacher/reader might think in each case. Regardless of whether you agree with the comments, take them seriously.

4. Insights

The authors of this book added comments after reviewing each essay and critique. These additional thoughts should help focus your thinking about a particular essay.

Topic A: Essays 1 and 2

> Should teachers reveal their political views to their classes? On the one hand, they may unfairly influence what their students think; on the other, if they're up-front about their own views, they may encourage students to talk more and be alert for any bias the teacher may have.
>
> **Assignment:** In your essay, take a position on this question. You may write about either one of the two points of view given, or you may present a different point of view on this question. Use specific reasons and examples to support your position.

Essay 1

For years students, teachers, administrators, and parents have struggled with the debate of whether or not teachers should reveal their political views to their classes. On one side of the issue, teachers introducing their personal political beliefs is seen as an abuse of power. In most cases, students are a captive audience in the classroom and many people think that teachers unfairly influence their pupils' views. However, if what Aristotle said, "that man by nature is a political animal," is true, then is it possible to separate politics from teaching? I think not.

While I recognize that every classroom should be a fair, unbiased environment, I also think that a little conflict can be a good thing. By introducing their political views, teachers not only personally invest themselves in class, but also stimulate discussion among other students. Conflict always sparks a student's attention and political debate is the perfect forum for a student to involve themselves in a class. Students can further develop their own identity by analyzing what political beliefs they agree or disagree with.

Moreover, teachers are more attentive and passionate about their teaching if they include their personal beliefs. There is nothing worse than sitting in a classroom staring at a teacher who is more bored by the subject matter than you are. When teachers are excited about what they teach, students are excited about what they learn.

Finally, I think it is unfair to say that teachers unfairly influence students' views. I believe that every student has the ability to think for him/herself and challenge ideas brought up in class. Learning is more than memorization. Learning is about testing, challenging, and discovering ideas.

In the final analysis, it is evident that teachers revealing their political views to their classes are not wrongfully brainwashing their students. Rather, through encouraging discussion and stimulating interest, teachers allow students to take ownership of their education and explore ideas otherwise untouched.

Critique

The author presents the issue in a complex and multifaceted way, recognizing the two sides of the issue and offering more than one argument in support of her position. Moreover, her essay is appropriately divided into fairly well-organized paragraphs. However, the thesis is not totally apparent, the arguments sometimes lack an essential link to the topic, and the writing is occasionally vague.

At the end of the author's introduction, the reader knows the author thinks it is OK for teachers to bring politics into the classroom, but it is unclear why the author thinks this. To support her position she quotes only Aristotle, which is not sufficient. A good thesis indicates a position and at least offers a preview of the support the author will provide in the body.

The next problem is the lack of a connection between the topic and the author's arguments. In the third paragraph, for instance, the author observes that teachers will do a better job if they are excited by what they are teaching. This may be true, but there are many ways for teachers to get excited about the subject matter they teach. The author does not show how bringing politics to the classroom is a unique way for teachers to get excited.

The final problem is vague writing. In the second paragraph, the author writes, "Students can further develop their own identity by analyzing what political beliefs they agree or disagree with." How students develop their identities through political argumentation is not obvious. This is an important aspect of the author's argument, and she must explain it more clearly.

The essay's structural integrity, generally good writing, and multiple points of view make it strong. A clearer thesis and better-developed arguments would make it stronger.

SCORE: 5–6

Insights

- To make this essay a 6, the thesis must be more clear. The author would need to make the argument about teachers being excited stronger—she must indicate that nothing makes teachers so excited as politics, and that therefore teaching their political views improves the quality of their teaching as nothing else could.
- Additionally, the second paragraph would have to be less vague.

Essay 2

Many young people do not watch the news or read newspapers. As a result of this, many form their political opinions based on the political opinions of their friends, families, and other influential people in their life. Some of the most influential people in a young person's life are their teachers. Teachers are seen by students as some of the most educated, well-informed, and respected people they know.

Students hold teachers in such high esteem that they are easily influenced by their opinions, especially their political opinions.

When teachers impose their political opinions onto students, even in just a joking manner or a single comment, those students will most likely adapt the political opinion of the teacher. If not take on the political opinion, it will at least affect their opinion in some way. Even if those teachers are not well-informed on the current political situation, the students will still believe and trust that the teachers are all-knowing.

Students should form their own political opinions and views. It is not appropriate for teachers to try to push their political views on students. Although these teachers may have the students' best interests in mind, the classroom should not be used to advance one's own political view.

Critique

Here the author chooses a relevant theme—the power imbalance between teachers and students—in addressing the question. In doing so, she lays the groundwork for what could be a compelling argument. However, her essay suffers from unwarranted claims, inadequate development, and a weak thesis.

The author is most culpable for offering assertions without evidence. She opens up by observing that young people learn about politics from influential adults. Fair enough, but then she implies that teachers are uniquely influential without providing support. Why are teachers most responsible for holding back on their political opinions? The author then writes that "[s]tudents . . . are easily influenced by [teachers'] opinions, especially their political opinions." Why politics especially? Finally, the author makes the extreme claim that students will "most likely adapt" teachers' opinions. Besides misusing the word "adapt," the student again fails to provide support.

The author's next two mistakes are related. First, she does not take her argument far enough. She argues that students are impressionable and will be swayed by their teacher's opinions, but she does not say why that matters. Second, she does not present her argument with a clear thesis early in the essay. The thesis appears in the last paragraph: "It is not appropriate for teachers to try to push their political views on students." But this is not enough because it does not answer the question, "So what?" A good argument cannot merely claim, "X will happen"; it must also relate the desirable or undesirable consequences of X.

The author does provide three complete paragraphs, each of which has the potential to contribute to a stronger essay. The lack of further evidence and a fuller, more incisive thesis prevent the essay from succeeding.

SCORE: 3–4

Insights

- Writing, we are often told, is a process of discovery. This essay is a case in point. The writer apparently "discovered" her true point only near the end of her essay. Nothing unusual in that. Writers often start writing without knowing what direction they're headed. Gradually, they begin to make connections and eventually arrive at a conclusion. That's no problem unless, as in this essay, the writer does not go back to fix the beginning. The lesson here is that you would do better to plan ahead: take about five minutes to think before you start writing. Anticipate your argument well enough that you can at least hint at the thesis in the first paragraph.
- Our critiquer compliments this writer for "laying the groundwork," and he's right. The writer slowly builds from point to point in a deductive line of reasoning that goes like this: (1) most young people are not informed; (2) therefore, they depend on their friends, families, and other influential people for their political views; and (3) teachers are some of

the most influential people in their lives. That logic is compelling and effective.

- The critiquer is a bit off base when he accuses the writer of implying that teachers are "uniquely influential," especially about "politics." In fact, the writer has specifically referred to friends and families as prime influences. What the writer only hints at, however, is that teachers bear a burden of responsibility to not abuse their positions of authority over their students—that ties into the writer's thesis and, as already mentioned, is an area of the paper that only emerges in the last paragraph.

Topic B: Essays 3 and 4

One of your friends, a senior like you, has decided to enlist in the Marine Corps after graduation. Another has been offered a job with his dad's company, and a third friend has decided to do some mission work for her church. You had been thinking about going to college, but now you wonder whether it might be smarter to take a year or two off. Is it best to go to college straight after high school (and keep up your academic momentum) or to take a year away before continuing your education?

Assignment: In your essay, take a position on this question. You may write about either one of the two points of view given, or you may present a different point of view on this question. Use specific reasons and examples to support your position.

Essay 3

Perhaps one of the most confusing times in an adolescent's life is the transition from high school to the next arena of one's life. Up until high school graduation, young people don't have many decisions to make concerning the course of their lives. What each high school senior decides to do after graduation is often times the first life-altering choice they had the opportunity to make. This can be a very stressful and confusing time in one's life and to complicate matters worse, everybody wants to inject their opinion. Your parents tell you to go straight to college. Your friends say to take some time off and think about what you want to do when you get older, and your guidance counselor tells you to "follow your heart"—whatever that means.

What's a kid to do? After seeing several of the upperclassmen graduate and move on to college, I would have to agree that not everyone is ready for "the college experience." With college comes much freedom and with much freedom comes a great deal of responsibility. Some students just aren't mature enough to handle these new responsibilities such as "time management," "developing healthy study habits," or perhaps, the best one—"drinking in moderation." For these students (you know who you are) I say wait a year or two before embarking in the doors of college life. I've seen too many older friends in my life go straight to college after high school simply b/c it was "the next step"—never mind their inability to manage their time, use healthy study habits, and not binge drink at college parties.

Yet although there is this crowd of individuals who should "take a year off" to mature, it is my recommendation that high school students not take time off.

I cannot begin to tell you how many of my older siblings or friend's older siblings have taken years off, pledging they will go back when they know what they want to do w/ their life—and never do. Once you get off the school treadmill, it's awfully difficult to get back on. Often times the student who says, "I'm going to take a year off," their year off turns into 2 yrs, 3 yrs, 4 yrs, and so on. Pretty soon they're 27 years old and working construction, watching their high school buddies get promoted in their careers.

Critique

This essay's greatest strength is its specific examples. Rather than just stating that there are dangers in going to college too early, the author enumerates several problems an ill-prepared student might encounter. Additionally, the author offers a couple of fairly well-structured paragraphs. However, the thesis is misplaced (in the middle of the essay), the grammar is often incorrect, and the overall structure of the essay is poor.

At the end of the author's very long first paragraph, it is still unclear what his position is. Then, after reading the second paragraph the reader might reasonably think the author opposes going straight to college, but the reader would be mistaken. Suddenly the thesis appears, as its own one-sentence paragraph in the middle of the essay. When a thesis is buried in the middle of an essay, a reader struggles to identify the author's position.

The thesis positioning creates structural problems, but the greater problem is that the essay ends without any sort of conclusion. The author claims that it is best to go straight to college, but he has not provided a coherent argument. He offers one set of observations concerning why it is best to wait and another set concerning why it is best not to wait, but he never provides the tie-breaking logic or evidence.

The final problem with the essay is that it is not very well written. The first paragraph is marked by repeated noun-pronoun disagreements as sentences switch back and forth from singular to plural. Then there is an illogical shift from third to second person at the end of the first paragraph. And often, the author misuses words, as in "embarking in the doors of college life." The author clearly has a point of view, and has perhaps convinced the reader that he is capable of producing a coherent argument. However, he has not completed the job and he has erred along the way.

SCORE: 3–4

Insights

- This essay shows a different problem with time. In Essay 2, we saw where not planning ahead led to a poor argument. Here, the writer runs out of time—his paper stops a paragraph or two before its natural conclusion. The writer probably didn't spend too much time planning, and he simply wasn't prepared to write out his essay in longhand. That effort may surprise you. Many students will find that their hands cramp up and their arms grow weary before they've run out of things to say. Practice writing for thirty minutes several times before the test to produce your best effort.

- The critiquer notes that the essay is "not very well written." One reason for that impression is that the writer is trying to sound very formal or academic by using language he's not completely comfortable with. For example, in the first sentence of the essay the writer uses "an adolescent's life," "the transition from high school," and "the next arena of one's life." Are any of these words or phrases common to what high school students talk and write about? Probably not. Don't try to impress anyone with your erudition or a world-class vocabulary. Instead, concentrate on trying to express yourself with simple diction and a clear purpose.

Essay 4

It is a decision that many young people are faced with. Should I continue with my academic career and go on to college or take a couple of years off to find myself and decide what I want in life? The decision may be easier than it sounds.

In today's society a college education is of great importance. The vast majority of well-paying jobs require an applicant to possess a four-year degree before they even take a second look. Some may argue that they plan to eventually go back to school and get a degree, but statistics show that many of these people never follow through. Not only will it be harder to get back into the academic mode of studying, but trying to attend college courses while working and raising a family can be nearly impossible.

Also, it should not be overlooked that a person can obtain the same if not a greater level of personal growth through the process of college as they would venturing off into the working world. After all, much of the college experience is about growth and finding one's place in the world. Also, it is possible to gain valuable work experience by maintaining a job while attending school. The answer to the question is clear. When faced with the fork in the road, go the right direction and go on to college.

Critique

The essay's greatest strength is that the author provides a complete answer to the question. Not only does she argue that it is beneficial to go straight to college, but she observes the potential detriments of not going. She also explains that the two options are mutually exclusive, since it is very hard to go back to college later in life. The essay would be better if it were better organized and if it presented its thesis earlier and more clearly. And some originality would help.

The author anticipates her thesis in the first paragraph, but does not provide it. She observes that "[t]he decision [whether to go to college] may be easier than it sounds," but she does not reveal what the decision should be until later. In crafting a well-structured argument in this format, suspense is not of much value. The essay would be stronger if the thesis came earlier, so that it could be developed and supported as the essay progresses.

Another problem is the essay's relatively poor organization. In the short second paragraph, the author argues in favor of a college education. Then she switches to arguing that students seldom return to school after leaving, and then she switches back to arguing the merits of going to college. The essay would be better—and easier to read—if each topic were dealt with comprehensively, one paragraph at a time.

A final problem is the author's fairly generic observations. She writes, "A college education is of great importance." This is not controversial, and it would not be necessary to disagree to argue on behalf of taking time off before college. Then she observes that balancing family, work, and school is exceedingly difficult. True, but everyone knows that; the author could have set the bar higher to craft a more convincing argument.

The author provides a thorough enough answer to the question and makes few errors, but a better essay would be clearer and better organized.

SCORE: 4

Insights

- Don't let yourself catch "it-itis." This is the unfortunate propensity to use "it" too much, especially at the beginning of a paper or essay. This writer begins her essay with "It is a decision . . ." forcing the reader to remind herself what "it" refers to. Go ahead and repeat some of the language in the question in your first paragraph. For example, this writer could have begun like this: "High school seniors are faced with what they think is a tough decision—whether to go on to college or not. That decision is easier than they think." A simpler beginning would look like this: "Many young people face this decision: should I continue with my academic career . . ."

- A larger problem with this essay is its lack of empathy. The writer does not seem able to reach beyond her own experience. She can't imagine, in other words, what compelling reasons a high school senior might have for not going straight to college. The ACT presents you with two sides of an issue: you're definitely expected to seize one side and argue it, but your argument will always be more persuasive if you make it clear you understand the alternative.

Topic C: Essays 5 and 6

Fights between players and fans have become common in professional sports. At your school, a group of basketball fans have been getting more and more outrageous with their "school spirit." The principal has threatened to ban them from all future games. After all, sports is about sportsmanship, but on the other hand, doesn't fan enthusiasm support school spirit? Where would you draw the line between acceptable and unacceptable fan behavior?

Assignment: In your essay, take a position on this question. You may write about either one of the two points of view given, or you may present a different point of view on this question. Use specific reasons and examples to support your position.

Essay 5

While many professional athletes state they are not role models, just as many sell their names on shoes, hats, wristbands, CDs, soft drinks, food, I could go on forever. Professional athletes are role models, but they are also people who need to be treated with respect from all, including fans.

School is a place for education on not only academics, but life as well. Although taunting rivals and playing mind games with players may be fun, sports are about proving who is the best. Fans are a part of that too. Fans excite, motavate, and support their teams. However, to truly prove that your team is the best, there is no reason to try and weasel out a win by making obnoxious and outragious gestures or remarks. School is a great place not only to teach, but demand respect from fans. Even with restrictions fans will be able to cheer on their team, but in a more appropriate way.

Because the students represent the school, just like the team, the principal has every right to bar the "spirited" group from games if he feels danger or unsportsmanlike behavior could taint the event. Unacceptable fan behavior consists of actions that harm or degrade the facility, other fans, officials, coaches, and players. Perfectly successful cheering can be accomplished without such acts.

Not just fans at professional events should be required to uphold sportsmanship. All fans in general from Little League to the World series should be expected rather required and demanded to show respect for not only the players, but more importantly, the game or sport itself.

Critique

The author provides some relevant observations regarding fan behavior. That fans represent the school as much as do the players, and thus deserve a venue to demonstrate their spirit, is an interesting idea that would contribute effectively to a complete essay. However, the author never quite provides that answer, and instead offers an essay characterized by poor organization and repeated errors.

The essay's thesis comes close to the end of the essay, where the author writes, "Unacceptable fan behavior consists of actions that harm or degrade the facility, other fans, officials, coaches, and players." This is a good start, but the question prompt asks about both acceptable and unacceptable behavior. The author mentions examples of each kind of behavior, but does not answer the question specifically enough. An effective thesis would be more precise and would come earlier in the essay.

Another problem is the introduction, which is essentially unrelated to the rest of the essay. The author never explains how professional athletes' endorsements are related to high school spirit. In fact, where she writes, "I could go on forever," she has already gone on for much too long.

The author's writing errors exacerbate the essay's weaknesses. Many of the sentences are structurally unsound and confusing, often from lack of proper punctuation, as in "should be expected rather required and demanded." Some words are grossly misspelled, including one ("outragious") that the author could have only looked to the question prompt to learn how to spell. Her content proves that she is capable of providing an interesting answer, but she does not deliver with her structure or her style.

SCORE: 3

Insights

- The critiquer faults this writer for using references to professional athletes, but he fails to see how those references help provide a structure for the essay. The writer begins with a reference to the status of pro athletes as role models. Although she doesn't say so, she could have made the point that just as high school athletes model their behavior on their older athletic heroes, high school fans do the same (and the fan behavior at NBA games can be awful). That keeps her reference to pro athletes from being as relevant as it might have been, but it does create a bookend, a place to anchor the beginning. She brings in the other bookend in the last paragraph when she refers to fans at professional events. The writer has now brought her argument full circle. The writer creates a sense of closure by using similar references at the beginning and end of her essay.

- The critiquer also misjudges the writer's thesis. He identifies it as "Unacceptable fan behavior consists of . . ." In fact, the essay's true thesis is this: "All fans should be expected, required and demanded to show respect." The writer is staking out a strong, unambiguous position, although as the critiquer rightly points out, she waits far too long to do so.

Essay 6

Are high school fans becoming too outrageous? Are they endangering the players or perhaps the other fans? I think not. Fans will be fans and I think the more outrageous and funny there antics are makes the game more exciting. But is there a line between acceptable fan behavior and unacceptable?

Yes, there is. We need to define this line and make it clear to all the fans, players, coaches, and officials. It is OK for fans to dress up funny and do comical things. I also believe it is okay to taunt the other team and make fun or even rag them. I think it's not okay when fans pick out a certain player, coach, or official and get on their back about there playing ability or just plain making jokes at them.

Players can only take so much verbal abuse, just like a regular human being. In fact, that's all they are, just people. Officials need to listen up to signs of too much abuse coming from the seats and when that fan crosses the line, then kick him out.

Fan behavior between high school, college, and pro leagues are different and should be treated so. High school fans rag the other players and team, but the athletes are so into the game they don't pay attention to it. So give them more leeway than you should to pro and college fans.

Overall, outrageous behavior by the fans makes the game more exciting and more interesting to watch. But players need to keep their cool and officials need to recognize when a fan goes too far. You can't blame the fans for everything.

Critique

The author has demonstrated, perhaps, that he understands the question, but not that he knows how to answer it. The essay offers only a vague description of what sort of fan behavior is inappropriate, without really explaining how or when to draw the line between acceptable and unacceptable. Additionally, the author's assertions are unsupported.

Roughly halfway through the essay, the author provides a semblance of a thesis: fans have crossed the line when they have begun to abuse the players. The author does not offer a set of criteria that determine what constitutes abuse. Is it verbal or physical abuse? Have players been abused when they have been rendered unable to play the game or merely when they have been insulted? The author provides some categories, such as "taunting" versus "ragging," but the difference between these categories is totally unclear.

Most of the essay's argumentation comes in the form of personal assertions. The author writes, "I think the more outrageous and funny there antics are makes the game more exciting," as if his private opinion is all the reader awaits. Later he says he thinks it's OK to tease players generally but not OK to isolate certain players. For his argument to be complete he needs to say why one behavior is OK and the other is not. To successfully argue that a behavior is bad, the author must illustrate the consequences of that behavior.

Here again, the author has laid out some of the content he might use to craft a compelling essay, but he has not used that content to his advantage.

SCORE: 2

Insights

- Here's a suggestion for this writer: make a list. Draw a line down the middle of a sheet of scratch paper (or the back of the ACT test booklet). On one side list acceptable fan behavior, at least according to your standards. On the other side, list unacceptable behavior. Now look over the list and organize your paper accordingly. As the essay stands, it's clear the writer launched into this project with little or no planning and no clear sense of direction. As a result, the essay is almost a hopeless muddle.

- The critiquer is right to point out how this writer seems to think his personal opinion is convincing by itself. Big mistake. You want to support your argument in more effective ways. For example, you could use an argument with emotional appeal—in this case, something like, "Let's not take the fun out of the game by gagging fans, but let's educate them on more appropriate ways to enjoy cheering." Seems reasonable, too. Or you could try a logical argument: "Players are people, too. Consider how you would like to be treated as a visitor in some other school's gym." Or if you were determined to make your argument personal, establish some credibility, for example: "I played on my high school team for three years and saw lots of crazy fan behavior— some funny in a good-natured way and some downright vicious."

Topic D: Essays 7 and 8

In an issue of a Maryland high school newspaper, letters were printed in response to an advertisement the newspaper had run for the Island Dreams Surf Station. Most of the letters were concerned that the ad portrayed the women as possessions. Furthermore, women were referred to in the ad as "chicks." One female student, who wrote the newspaper with an opposing view, said, "Island Dreams is a surf shop that sells *bathing suits*. The ad was simply trying to market their products." Another female student wrote that the critical comments were "absurd." After all, it's "advertising." Do you believe that high school newspapers should have limits placed on their First Amendment rights?

Assignment: In your essay, take a position on this question. You may write about either one of the two points of view given, or you may present a different point of view on this question. Use specific reasons and examples to support your position.

Essay 7

The first amendment is one of America's most valued rights. Freedom of speech and freedom of the press remain absolutely critical factors in upholding a free society. These rights give individuals the opportunity to voice their ideas and opinions without fear of government censorship. However, in an institution such as a school, limits must be set for student journalists and advertisers because younger people may not always set the limits for themselves.

I say this not because I believe that students should be kept under strict watch of the types of ideas they have; on the contrary I think that expressing opinions is crucial in fostering a healthy learning environment. I also believe that all kids should learn about their individual rights such as the freedom of speech, but people who have a large influence in a school community, such as student journalists, need to understand that they are producing work for impressionable kids and some amount of civility and tact must be used when expressing their thoughts to the public. For instance, even many college students are insulted when a gentlemen's show club advertises in the university newspaper. These students are easily influenced and furthermore, easily offended, which is not (hopefully) the aim of a high school newspaper.

When teachers show movies in class, they must be tasteful; when a school invites a speaker to lecture or give a presentation, the content may be controversial, but must be non-offensive to the entire student body; and high school newspapers, though they are created by the students, are no exception to this censorship in schools. By no means am I suggesting that students should be kept from becoming informed on contentious issues, but how they are becoming informed must be non-offensive.

In conclusion, I believe that limits should be placed on high school newspapers, because restrictions need to be set for young individuals who might not set them for themselves. Certainly the "real world" has more freedom, but it also has a great deal more responsibility. I think that a well produced school newspaper reflects in itself a responsible student body, but certain restrictions in school help students mature and therefore lead them to make their own choices and set their own limits when they finally reach the "real world." But that's just my opinion.

Critique

The author has written an essay that clearly addresses the question, presents a point of view, and attempts to support that point of view in relatively well-structured paragraphs. Moreover, she has done so in clear, error-free prose. However, her argument lacks sufficient support and her ideas do not stay consistent throughout.

The first three sentences of the essay are useless platitudes—the essay would be much stronger if its fourth sentence, the thesis, came first. The thesis is clear, but the body does a poor job of supporting the thesis. The author's main idea is that students must have restrictions imposed on them because they will not restrict themselves. Unfortunately, paragraphs two and three have nothing to do with this idea; they only deal with why some level of censorship is important. They suggest that limitations are good, but do not support the author's thesis that young students will not limit themselves.

An additional problem is that the author does not really provide a complete argument as to why the limitations are good. She writes that students are impressionable, but she does not prove that students' impressionability is a sufficient reason to limit their freedom of speech. That students are easily influenced is not itself an argument; it is merely a premise in an argument that does not appear in this essay.

The closest thing to a cohesive argument in this essay comes in the final paragraph, where the author suggests that since students don't really have responsibilities in the real world, they do not deserve First Amendment protection. This is the beginning of a good argument, and one that supports the author's thesis, but it comes too late in the essay to be effective. The essay is structurally sound and generally well written, but it suffers logically by failing to support its own argument.

SCORE: 4

Insights

- The writer of this essay should have spent more time outlining her essay in her head before putting pen to paper. Brainstorming two or three specific examples to support the thesis would have made the argument seem less thin. A passing reference to a "gentleman's show club" is not sufficient support, not to mention the negative impression that an evaluator might form of the writer.
- The critique correctly points out that the thesis would be better as the first sentence. Avoid empty generalizations as a substitute for a compelling introductory sentence. First impressions do matter, especially when the evaluators will be quickly skimming the essays.

- The essay is needlessly repetitive. Think of developing your arguments in depth instead. You might try referring to the specific quotes in the prompt as an initial strategy.

Essay 8

"You terrorist" muttered one of my classmates to another one. The boy had directed this comment, in the weeks after September 11, towards another classmate who was Gujarati. Perhaps this boy had uttered those words out of pain, or maybe his parents hadn't properly taught him about manners, or maybe he learned by example, watched television and observed the racial belittlement of others by bigger bullies. Whatever the case, he was unaware what devastating pain he had caused to the boy who was Gujarati, and even unaware that what he said was unacceptable and wrong. It was only after the Dean of our division personally talked to the insulter and informed him of the consequences of his comment, and blatantly stated that what he had said was wrong, did the boy understand that he could not get away with making derogatory racial generalizations.

To me, high school should represent an educational facility that fosters an open learning atmosphere but also a safe haven for its students. Although the purpose of an education is to learn about a variety of different subjects, it is not necessary to expose adolescents to everything. While school newspapers are meant to be informative and involve students in the outside community, they should still be censored to a certain degree. It is essential to place some limits on a high school newspaper's first amendment rights because of the diversity of students at school and high schools should not mirror all of society's habits and norms.

Without putting much effort into it, you can now learn almost a whole new language of disparaging and hurtful slang that can be directed towards others. Unfortunately this behavior is encouraged and even rewarded in magazines, on the Internet and on television, perhaps with the exception of PBS. A diverse populace of students is enrolled in every high school, all of whom come from different backgrounds with varying cultural and familial values. Because of this diversity, high school newspapers must use some form of censorship to keep the articles informative, not offensive. Newspapers should still be able to write about controversial subjects but must remain objective and avoid any underlying judgment. For instance, a student journalist at my high school wrote an article on the constant false accusations and racial libel that citizens of Middle Eastern descent, living in the United States, were forced to endure directly following September 11th. Instead of encouraging this behavior, the article addressed why this was happening, it addressed the emotions of both the insulter and insulted, and suggested some solutions to the problem.

Although the Island Dreams Surf Station Ad was advertising bathing suits, it was not necessary to refer to the women modeling the suits as chicks. The term "chicks" encourages deprecation of women and suggests they are not as good as men. School newspapers should not be using nor encouraging the use of slang as children might think it is acceptable. High school needs to remain a place where students can express themselves without condemnation or insult, where they can learn and where they can develop good habits. Like we are constantly reminded, children are the future, so school newspapers and global media alike need to set a good example for how those children should act in the future. By accomplishing this, instead of degrading people for their cultural differences, we might be able to embrace this diversity and expand our horizons.

Critique

The author presents four fairly well-organized paragraphs, and each paragraph presents an observation or example relevant to the question. The author thus proves his understanding of the question. He also presents a point of view—limitations are good—but his thesis is unclear and poorly supported.

The opening paragraph is interesting, but it is a bit too long since it is not completely relevant to the question. The thesis comes in the second paragraph and it is quite unclear. The author argues that First Amendment limitations are good because "the diversity of students at schools and high schools should not mirror all of society's habits and norms." Since the author does not adequately describe "society's habits and norms" or explain what it means for a school's diversity to mirror those norms, the thesis is confusing.

The third paragraph presents a different sort of argument: student newspapers must be restricted so that they do not offend the sensitivities of schools' diverse populations. This is a fair argument, but it is not one that evidently supports the author's thesis. Another problem with the third paragraph is its overgeneralizations. The author writes that a "diverse populace of students is enrolled in every high school." This is not true; many high schools have a homogenous populace. This problem does not significantly affect the author's argument, but any hyperbolized, unsupported assertion weakens the essay.

Another problem with the third paragraph is that it does not answer the question specifically enough. The question asks whether high school newspapers should have First Amendment limitations placed on them, and the author responds by saying they should because high schools are diverse. This argument could work anywhere. Should municipal newspapers have limitations because cities are diverse? Should corporate newsletters have limitations because businesses are diverse? The author argues that limitations are good without really arguing why limitations are good at high schools.

The final paragraph is OK in itself, but does not quite relate to the thesis or to the third paragraph. The author of this essay has some good ideas and some well-organized paragraphs, but the essay as a whole suffers from an ongoing lack of clarity.

SCORE: 4

Insights

- This essay is an excellent example of what can happen to a bright student who doesn't understand how to structure an argument. If you outline your argument before beginning to write, you can avoid some of the inconsistencies.
- A strength of this essay is linking the argument to the specifics mentioned in the prompt. The "chicks" reference, however, would have been more compelling if juxtaposed against the "terrorist" comment in the opening. That comparison might have provided a better framework for developing the essay.
- The introduction was especially effective. From the verb choice "muttered" to the timeliness of terrorism in our lives, the writer makes us want to read on.

Topic E: Essays 9 and 10

Many students think of the Summer Job as something parents make you do. In the *Washington Post*, Elizabeth Kastor asserted that it is "the way you learn that work is tedious." Other adults wax nostalgic about what they learned on their first summer jobs—of course, they are looking back after many years of forgetting. Some psychologists suggest that work comes too quickly for young people. These psychologists argue that the time would be better spent in holding on to childhood. Do you believe that summer jobs have value?

Assignment: In your essay, take a position on this question. You may write about either one of the two points of view given, or you may present a different point of view on this question. Use specific reasons and examples to support your position.

Essay 9

Summer jobs, rather than being some form of deprivation, I believe do nothing but enhance the lives of those of us fortunate enough to locate employment on a part-time basis. Even though employed, there seems to be plenty of play moments in most cases.

I learned this valuable lesson from talking to my grandmother. Besides the feeling of pride in earning spending money without having to go to my parents for every treat, just knowing one is being a productive individual should be an incentive to wish to contribute in whatever capacity is available.

Expecting an opportunity to find and maintain a summer job in the early 1940s, according to my grandmother, was considered a rare privilege, as demand for part-time employment was high. 1943, with World War II in full swing, opened up replacement jobs. These jobs were to replace the young men who went off to defend our country. Furthermore, the depression years were ending. With adult men and women working in defense plants, and young men in military service, both full and part-time employment was becoming a reality for young people.

Five dollars a week for Grandmother seemed to be almost more than she could hope for, when she was offered a job in a grocery store. Not quite fourteen years old, this opportunity afforded a sudden feeling of "pre-adulthood" for her, as she could now contribute to the cost of tuition for a coveted high school she wished to attend. Out of range for her parents to provide without some help—given her father's meager income—Grandmother was happy to work nine hours each day for the summer months. An occasional ice cream treat by her employer was a welcome bonus.

The next three summers, as more young men came of age and were called to serve, more job vacancies were created. And although there seemed to be more opportunities, relatives and close friends were the first considered for those jobs. Grandmother was fortunate once more to find work in a grocery store. But this time for real hourly wages. Twenty-five cents an hour was the going wage, and since there was no limit to the hours allowed for teens then, the pay seemed like a windfall.

The duties Grandmother was expected to fulfill included filling orders taken by phone, boxing groceries to be delivered, stocking shelves, cleaning vegetable and bakery cases, and serving customers who showed up at the door to shop by asking for products and having them located and bagged.

The education Grandmother gleaned from these experiences were invaluable. A work ethic, which persists to this day, learning the value of money, and a feeling of contribution all figure into her personality.

You can learn a lot from your grandmother if you just listen. From what I've learned, a job, no matter in what capacity, nor what recompense, is never a fruitless endeavor.

Critique

The author has a clear point of view: summer jobs do have value. The author also chooses a pertinent example to support her point of view; anecdotal evidence can be highly effective. The essay, however, is logically weak.

The author's only real argument seems to be that summer jobs must be valuable in general because her grandmother's summer job was valuable, but the author gives the reader no reason to believe that other part-time employees will benefit in the same way her grandmother benefited. The problem is exacerbated by the fact that the author's grandmother was put to work more than a half-century ago, and the author doesn't even attempt to argue why what was valuable in 1945 will be valuable in 2005. A detailed example can effectively support an argument; here the author uses one in place of an argument.

Another problem with the essay is that it fails to address the complexity of the question. The author ignores the reality that some work is tedious. She might have chosen to argue that summer jobs are valuable despite their being tedious, but instead she just does not address the objection. This is doubly bad given that her grandmother's job sounds especially tedious. The author also ignores the psychologists' argument that some people are put to work too early.

Here again it matters that her grandmother worked during World War II—could what was a working age then be too young today? The author is not expected to address all of these complexities, but using one example to answer such a broad question is much too simple.

Despite some problems, the essay is ultimately clear and well organized, and the author's point of view is understandable and consistent.

SCORE: 5

Insights

- Using your grandmother as an example is an excellent strategy. The fact that the writer remembers so much of what her grandmother said has to be endearing to almost any reader. If the reader loves his grandmother too, you are likely to benefit from that affection.
- The critiquer correctly points out the narrowness of scope and the lack of timeliness. You should have at least two examples to support your position. Don't, however, believe that three are necessary (as some prep books and the five-

paragraph essay might lead you to think). A weak third example is far worse than not fulfilling some arbitrary expectation on the part of a reader.

· The true strength of this essay is that you find yourself liking the writer. If the reader likes you, do you think that your score might be higher? It's very hard not to love Grandma....

Essay 10

Summer jobs may have value and they may not, depending on who is experiencing the early mornings guarding lives poolside, late nights sitting as a baby sleeps, or greasy days serving food. Everybody is different. Each child is unique. Special gifts, talents, and idiosyncrasies grace each human life. Developmental psychology research discusses three temperaments noticeable at birth that are innate, biological. Some babies are passive, easily pleased, others cannot be soothed. These temperaments develop as children grow, through maturation and experiences within their environment.

A fifteen-year-old may not have the self-awareness or the maturity level necessary to take responsibility for a job. He may find himself in an environment that is not a good fit, one that hinders his individual growth, stunts his self-efficacy. Authority can push and pull in many directions. Another individual, who "has it in her blood"; at thirteen years old may discover a drive, a trait that allows her to gain from a traditional work environment. She may steal her self-esteem from the ice cream parlor.

Is it expected that a teenager realize the possible value of having a summer job? Do they know that responsibility might feel good on them, that friends can be found in unexpected places, that work can get in the way of play, that money can be spent unwisely? Young people have a lot to think about, mostly themselves. They have to, consciously and not, decide if they are worth attention and from whom, consider the statement of their clothing, understand why they feel so strongly, and realize how confusion spins. Although developmentally shortsighted, young people can absorb the actions and attitudes of others.

Parents can help shape and discern the readiness of their teen for a summer job. They can help give it meaning. They can bumper harsh edges when needed, push or pull when their child seems stuck. Maybe this is the difference between Kastor's views of a summer job, too early and at a cost, and the nostalgic learning experience. Are work ethic, parent involvement, and acceptance of responsibility a thing of the past? Is the idea of parents wanting the best for their children and getting involved asking too much?

We are transformed through our environments, though they are not all powerful. Although one's personality is malleable, molding to circumstance, temperament is seen as relatively consistent. Try forcing a round peg into a square hole; especially before it has been exposed to the world, before it has gained a stable identity, before it is capable, if forced through, to regain its shape. Some teenagers will flourish in the light of a summer job, others will grow bitter. The importance is in realizing the individual.

Critique

The author has produced a well-developed essay; she does an excellent job of presenting a clear point of view early on and then elaborating on it and supporting it throughout. In the first sentence the author takes a position and in the remainder of the paragraph she explains her position. The explanation is essential to a good essay, as an acceptable answer is not: summer jobs have value. It is the author's burden to say specifically why summer jobs do or do not have value.

The author also presents solid support. Her thesis is that summer jobs have value for some children but not for others, and she presents clear examples of the type of children who are likely and unlikely to benefit from jobs. Additionally, the author uses both logic and evidence. Too often, writers provide the logic of why something should be the case without providing evidence that indicates that it actually is the case. Or they provide evidence that indicates that something is so without logically explaining why it is so. A good writer does both, as this one has done.

On the down side, the sentence quality is uneven and the essay is occasionally unclear. This problem persists and is compounded by errors in grammar, as in "before it is capable . . . to regain its shape." The author does a good job of varying the length of her sentences, but too many of the longer sentences are awkward and incorrect.

The lack of clarity exists sometimes at the sentence level and sometimes at the paragraph level. In the first paragraph the author refers to developmental psychology's three temperaments without explaining what those temperaments are. At the beginning of the fifth paragraph the author writes, "We are transformed through our environments, though they are not all powerful." Does she mean that not all environments are powerful or that environments are not omnipotent? The third paragraph is mostly a general discussion of the challenges that young people face, something that is not clearly related to the thesis that some summer jobs have value and some don't.

Overall the essay is first-rate. The author fulfills the writing task by answering the question in a clear and specific way and presenting well-organized paragraphs. The lapses in clarity and sentence quality, though, cause the essay to suffer somewhat.

SCORE: 6

Insights

- This essay may be uneven but the intelligence behind the ideas is undeniable. Most readers will not take the time to analyze each sentence as did the evaluator in this book. From the concrete details in the opening salvo to the power of the concluding sentence, you know that this is a thinker to be reckoned with. Phrases like "greasy days serving food" set her apart from her peers.

- Few high school students would be able to discuss this prompt in terms of developmental psychology. If you have expertise in a particular area, always ask yourself if you can apply that knowledge to the specific prompt. After all, sometimes it pays to be Jung at heart.

- Other than saying that there are "three temperaments" and not explaining what they are, this essay is an excellent model for you to study. The structure and content are superior.

Topic F: Essays 11 and 12

Some have said that we live in an Age of Apology. After a Monday Night Football pregame show featured partial nudity, Disney/ABC, a "family entertainment company," "apologized" all the way to the bank. The National Football League apologized as well but claimed that it knew nothing about its own pregame show. Many TV viewers say they are outraged by what they see on television, but continue to watch the same programs they criticize. And the networks point out that offended TV viewers can use their remotes to end taste malfunctions. Still, is saying you're sorry just a convenient means to avoid taking responsibility?

Assignment: In your essay, take a position on this question. You may write about either one of the two points of view given, or you may present a different point of view on this question. Use specific reasons and examples to support your position.

Essay 11

It's clear that the "family entertainment company" had anything but the family in mind when it claimed not to know what was on their own pre-game show. Primetime television is now infamous for its racy, risqué and raunchy programming, something not only unique to Disney/ABC. But, it is the apology afterward that reveals an even greater malady in our society. By dismissing this egregious error as a simple mistake, this company took advantage of its viewers, and the next week continued its inappropriate programming. Because of this example and the many others behind it, saying your sorry clearly is just a convenient means to avoid taking responsibility. This is the case especially if the apology is not reciprocated by other meaningful actions.

First, apologizing alone doesn't ameliorate the problem. You often times need an admission of guilt to crystallize an apology. For example, Former President Bill Clinton, after he left office, apologized for not urging more rapid action in Rwanda to end the genocide there that killed more than 800,000 people. He admitted fault and said that he should have done more to help the Rwandans. President Clinton also recommended to the United Nations that it set up a war crimes tribunal to bring the killers to justice. Apologizing isn't only saying you're sorry, it is also admitting guilt and doing something to fix the problem at hand. If Disney/ABC had admitted that it did something wrong and if it actually altered their programming, then the apology would have been sincere. Unfortunately, the company avoided taking responsibility by merely saying it's sorry.

Second, appearances matter. You can only say sorry as a convenient means of avoiding responsibility if the person you're apologizing to believes you. For example, in the recent Scott Peterson double murder case in California, people have had difficulty figuring out whether Scott is in fact sorry about his wife and child's deaths. Now regardless of whether he actually is, there are people who don't trust his word because he has already been tried in the court of public opinion. So accordingly, when Scott apologized, people automatically perceived otherwise. Many times, saying your sorry alone just doesn't cut it. Scott Peterson and Disney/ABC could have avoided the possibility of people not believing their apologies. They could have reciprocated them with some meaningful action. Even if they weren't trying to avoid taking responsibility, they appeared as they were.

Regrettably, we do live in an Age of Apology. But thankfully, we do have a way out. We must say we're sorry and still go further to ameliorate the underlying reason for the apology. This way, people will know that we are actually sincere. If we don't, then saying we're sorry will remain a convenient means to avoid taking responsibility.

Critique

The essay is well composed. The author presents a clear point of view, which she supports consistently and effectively throughout the essay. Moreover, the author provides thorough support, using both logic and evidence. For instance, in the second paragraph the author argues that words alone are ineffective because only actions bring about real change, and then she provides relevant examples. The essay's weaknesses are its inconsistent and erroneous uses of language and its redundancy.

The greatest language problem comes in the second paragraph. The author begins by writing, "apologizing alone doesn't ameliorate the problem." In addition to misusing the word "ameliorate" in this sentence, the author suggests that "apologizing" is the simple act of saying you're sorry. Later, however, the author claims, "Apologizing isn't only saying you're sorry." The author switches back and forth between arguing that apologizing is not enough and arguing that apologizing involves both words and actions. By the end of the paragraph, it is unclear whether "apologizing" and "saying sorry" are the same or different. Since apology is the whole subject of the essay, this point of confusion is problematic. Of lesser importance, the author misuses the word "reciprocate."

The next problem is that the third paragraph makes the same argument as the second paragraph. The author opens paragraph three with, "Second, appearances matter" as if she is introducing a new argument. Ultimately, however, the argument is a reiteration of the argument from the previous paragraph: words alone are not enough, so actions are needed too. The essay prompt did not demand multiple arguments, but masking one argument as two is unacceptable. Another problem in this paragraph is a lack of clarity. The author argues that Scott Petersen should have backed up his apology for murdering his wife and daughter with meaningful action. What, the reader might wonder, could he have done?

The essay succeeds because of its clear and consistent point of view and its well-developed argument. It would be even better if the author had a tighter grasp of language.

SCORE: 4

Insights

- This essay's strength is in having familiar examples. Although these examples are misapplied in the context of her argument, most readers who are skimming would probably buy that former president Clinton and Scott Peterson should have been more "sincere" in their apologizing. But it is risky to rely on intuitively persuasive responses from your readers. The reader might suddenly stop and think. So, therefore, should you.

- The critiquer correctly chastises the student for mangling language. Avoid overwriting. Better to be clear than to—as Rocky and Bullwinkle once said—"bandy about boisterous badinage." If you use words like "reciprocate" incorrectly, the reader might reciprocate with a lower score.

Essay 12

The forest floor is surprisingly dark, nearly black, though it is emblazoned with streaks of white and yellow. The trees overhead are cold, almost metallic in appearance, with a flickering glow casting a foggy halo nearby. Enormous cliffs, sharp peaks against the darkening sky, lean menacingly overhead, dwarfing the creatures roaming below. They shuffle purposefully by, a homogeneous mass moving as one. Others, alone, pace uncomfortably, eyes darting wildly, evaluating the fitness of the passing herd. Scavengers lurk in the waning light, monitoring the actions of predators nearby.

We are witness to the corporate wilderness; the Age of Apology is now. To a corporation, survival results from monetary success. Hence, the issuance of an apology is used as an economic tool. The apology, made after knowingly committing an unlawful or immoral act, is a measure taken to ease the predictably resulting outrage; it is a free pass for a free market. If the revenue generated by acting in a manner necessitating an apology is greater than that lost by offending consumers, the corporate board must necessarily choose the path of greatest profits. Corporate responsibility is many-faceted, but the bottom line ultimately trumps all. Its image may be temporarily tarnished or permanently scarred, but the company survives the dark night and sees the next day.

Unfortunately, the apology is an evasive maneuver which demonstrates waning effectiveness. An economic concept emphasized in every financial forum, whether Econ 101 at the community college or a Federal Reserve meeting, is the law of diminishing marginal returns. Simply stated, each additional unit of any commodity used provides the consumer less utility, or satisfaction, than the previous one. Similarly, each apology issued is less effective than the one before.

Every time Disney slaps itself on the wrist in a performance of public penance, fewer people believe the charade.

The apology acts as an excuse, a personal and public rationalization for an unwise course of action. More essentially, the tendency towards apology is a means of self-preservation. In times of carefree success, rational thought and higher reasoning govern action. But when the continuation of existence is in doubt, instinct comes to the fore. Knowingly or not, an apology is a desperate measure.

In the unforgiving ecosystem that is corporate competition, survival of the fittest reigns in a manner that would make Charles Darwin giggle with self-important delight. Nowhere else are the weak or dying more systematically eradicated. Nowhere else is evolution more apparent or more pervasive. As corporate executives roam fertile valleys made prosperous by the advertising dollar, those who stride carefully in the face of danger will live and grow and prosper. Those who are careless, resorting to frantic requests for forgiveness, will be kindly absolved, then promptly eaten.

Critique

The essay addresses the question only in part. The author presents one paragraph that deals squarely with the question, and impressively so; his argument is both creative and sound. However, the author strays off topic and his essay suffers.

The first paragraph is unclear, overwrought, and essentially irrelevant. The essay thus effectively begins in the second paragraph, where the author crafts an interesting and well-developed argument. He explains clearly why corporations apologize for actions and specifically how those apologies are designed to absolve the offenders of responsibility. The author thus provides a clear answer to the question. Though the second paragraph answer is good, it alone is not enough. The author responds to a relatively broad question by way of a single example.

The rest of the essay is irrelevant to the question. Instead of writing about whether apologies take the place of responsibility, he argues that the corporate apology is indicative of corporate failure. The question prompt is about apologies, not about corporate performance. Worse, the author's argument about how corporations use apologies is inconsistent. First, he writes that apologies result in monetary success, which results in survival. Then, he says that apologies demonstrate waning effectiveness. To argue his point, he talks about the diminishing marginal returns of apologies, and concludes that a single apology is an act of desperation. Unfortunately, the marginal returns analogy only indicates that several apologies are ineffective, not that a single one is. The author thus never justifies his conclusion.

The essay is not uninteresting, but it is self-indulgent; the author uses hyperbolized language in place of effective logic. He meanders his way to the heart of the question by the second paragraph, only to move away from it again in the third. The author's facility with language and command of logic is impressive, but here he has misdirected his gifts.

SCORE: 5

Insights

- This essay and critique clearly demonstrate what concerns many English teachers about the subjective nature of the ACT essay. In this case, the evaluator is missing the Forrester (if I may be self-indulgent enough to make a film reference) for the trees. The talent of this writer far outweighs the quibbling attacks on his approach. And sometimes, the evaluator is simply wrong. It is possible for corporations to apologize in order to achieve "monetary success" while, at the same time, those apologies are experiencing "waning effectiveness." The writer is not inconsistent, as the evaluator implies.

- The evaluator describes the first paragraph as "overwrought" and "irrelevant." And perhaps it suffers from a flabby adjective or two. On the other hand, the writer's facility with language separates this effort from the formulaic approach that most students will employ. After reading several hundred essays that open with a predictable thesis statement, is it difficult to believe that this writer will be rewarded for his creativity?

About the Authors

Randall McCutcheon, nationally recognized by the U.S. Department of Education for innovation in curriculum, has authored eight books, including *Can You Find It?*, a guide to teaching research skills to high school students, which received the 1990 Ben Franklin Award for best self-help book of the year; *Get Off My Brain*, a survival guide for students who hate to study, which was selected by the New York Public Library as one of 1998's Best Books for Teenagers; and three textbooks for speech and journalism courses.

After nearly a decade working in radio and television, McCutcheon taught for twenty-seven years in both public and private schools in Iowa, Massachusetts, Nebraska, and New Mexico. He was selected the State Teacher of the Year in Nebraska in 1985, and in 1987 he was named the National Forensic League National Coach of the Year. Elected to the N.F.L. Hall of Fame in 2001, he concluded a successful career as a high school speech coach. In twenty-seven years, his speech teams won twenty-five state and five national championships.

James Schaffer is the chair of the English Department at Nebraska Wesleyan University where he teaches writing and journalism courses. He has a Ph.D. in English from the University of Virginia and has been frequently involved in developing writing curricula, assisting with a freshman writing program, and leading writing workshops. He is the author of three textbooks and numerous articles.

Schaffer was a finalist for the Teacher-in-Space program in 1985 and, as a result, became a speaker and presenter for NASA. He has given more than four hundred programs on the space shuttle to professional organizations, community groups, and schools. He was named Nebraska's Aerospace Educator of the Year.

As a journalism advisor, he has lead his publication's staffs to numerous state and national awards, including the Best Magazine of the Year award from the Columbia Scholastic Press Association. Schaffer and his wife, Mary Lynn, also an educator, have three children—Suzanne, Sarah, and Stephen.